KARTING!

A COMPLETE INTRODUCTION

For the Prospective Karter

Jean L. Genibrel

Genibrel Publications

(562) 498-8172

© 1999 Genibrel Publications

5318 East Second Street, Suite 747
Long Beach, California 90803
(562) 498-8172

ISBN 0-9669120-0-4
10 9 8 7 6 5 4 3 2

DESIGN/PRINTING CREDITS

Cover design by Stan Goldstein. Interior design by Daniel Moran. Printed by Diversified Printers, Inc. of La Mirada, Ca.

PHOTO CREDITS

Debbie Unglert, WKA, IKF, KART, ISN Canada, Performance Karting News, National Kart News, Hot Shot Photography, JM Racing, Go Racing, Rock Island Grand Prix, Buller Built, Pitts Performance, KMI, and the author.

NOTICE

The information contained in this book is true and correct to the best of our knowledge. All recommendations and suggestion in this book and all the Genibrel Publications books are made without any guarantees on the part of the author and publisher. Some names used in this book are the property of the trademark owners and the use of such names does not imply endorsement and are used for identification purposes only. This is not an official publication. Karting is a dangerous sport and should only be practiced on approved properties and while wearing appropriate safety equipment. Be constantly aware that karting can be dangerous and injuries can occur. Because the use of the information contained in this book is beyond the control of the author and publisher, liability for such use is expressly disclaimed.

TABLE OF CONTENTS

1 KARTING TODAY 1

2 KARTING AND YOU 5

3 TWO AND FOUR-CYCLES 9

4 ENGINES 13

5 KART FRAMES 19

6 CLASSES AND RULES 25

7 CLUTCHES, LUBES, CHAINS 31

8 APPAREL AND SAFETY EQUIPMENT 34

9 ACCESSORIES, TOOLS, SPARES 39

10 USED CHASSIS 42

11 SCHOOLS, TRACKS, CLUBS & SHOPS 48

12 LISTS AND QUICK TIPS 53

FREQUENTLY ASKED QUESTIONS 55

SUPPLIERS 57

ABOUT THE AUTHOR

Born in France and raised in Canada, Jean Genibrel has made the U.S. his home since 1964. The author began his racing career in 1968 with an Austin Healy Sprite in local events. Later, Genibrel drove a Mini-Stock for a local team and received his first SCCA license racing a Gordini. Genibrel worked for several professional teams, notably Dan Gurney's All American Racers in the Bobby Unser and Jerry Grant days, Dick Guldstrand Enterprises, and many other SCCA, IMSA and Trans Am Teams. Jean built and raced several record setting project cars and engines for various teams and publications, ranging from Stock Cars, to karts and SCCA sedans.

Jean Genibrel has five books to his credit and has collaborated on three more as an editor for "Steve Smith Autosports Publications". Genibrel began racing karts in 1982 at Ascot Park in Gardena, California, and he has raced karts on most of the tracks in the southwest. Jean was president of the San Fernando Valley Kart Club in the mid '80s.

Jean Genibrel is best known for his karting publications, *The Beginner's Complete Karting Guide, Racing the Yamaha KT100S* and *4-Cycle Karting Technology,* which he co authored. Since 1982 Jean has been contributing editor to *National Kart News, Karttech, Circle Track, Short Track Racing, Sport Compact Car, Popular Hot Rodding, Stock Car Racing,* and *Bracket Racing USA.* Genibrel was the tech editor of *Rod Action & Street Machines* and most recently created, produced and edited *Kart Racer* magazine. In May 1998, Jean was the first journalist awarded for a karting story. Genibrel received the STP award at the 1998 Indy 500 banquet of the American Auto Racing Writers & Broadcasters Association.

The author/publisher is scheduled to produce a complete library of karting books, software and videos. Some of the books will be translated into French and others will be translated into Japanese and Spanish.

ACKNOWLEDGMENTS

Tom Argy Jr., John Bigelow, Kurt Burris, Kermit Buller, Dale Council, Dave Dimond, Ron and Linda Emmick, Cameron Evans, Doug Fleming, Fred Gerrior, Stan Goldstein, Rich Hlaves, Rich Hearn, Larry LaCost Jr., Jean Marchioni, Pete Muller, Dan Moran, Sven Pruett, Cal Karts, Invader, Taylor Nabokov, Go Racing Magazine, Pitts Performance, National Kart News, WKA, Adams Kart Track, So Cal Sprinters, Rock Island Grand Prix, IKF, KART, KMI, ISN Canada, and the guys on the Muller Karting List.

INTRODUCTION

Karting! A Complete Introduction was written to assist the prospective karter in choosing the appropriate division, class, engine and kart to fit his needs, desires and aspirations. Most importantly, the book will guide the novice in purchasing the appropriate equipment for his application, so he can be free to concentrate on learning how to drive competitively and on mastering the tuning of his chassis and engine.

This book was written for those who have a desire to enter the sport of kart racing in the most affordable, effortless and carefree manner, avoiding the pitfalls which can divert from the learning experience. Whether one aspires to lofty professional motorsports goals, or simply wants to race as a hobby, *Karting! A Complete Introduction* will usher the novice who is contemplating to enter karting, through the first steps of his new sport: the purchase of the equipment and the choice of a division and class. This is not an engineering book, nor a "how to go fast in karting" book, but rather a "how to get into karting easily, safely and economically" book. Learning from the mistakes many others have made, newcomers can learn the basics of the sport, rather than learning how to correct mistakes.

Karting is easy to get into and it looks so deceivingly so watching others race, that many newcomers over estimate their abilities and once they run a few races, they quickly realize that they have much to learn. Just like any other sport, karting has its own learning curve to follow. Could you imagine trying to play professional golf without any training? How about trying to become an Olympic gymnast in just a year or two. Or worse yet, with the wrong equipment or training? How different are those scenarios from a new karter expecting to win a championship in a couple years with the wrong kart? This volume, and the ones this publisher produces, prepare the karter to enter the learning curve ahead so he can keep steadfast in his apprenticeship. All this, in turn, will create a professional, competitive and faithful karter who in a couple of years can travel to any karting venue and compete with the best of them.

Novices typically have numerous questions before choosing their equipment, class, engine and division of karting. *Karting! A Complete Introduction* has two goals: To raise the questions American and Canadian newcomers should ask, and to answer them. These are the questions which experience has shown to be the ones to ask, rather than have the answers come up after the equipment has been purchased: "Which form of karting is right for me?," or "What type of engine do I prefer?," or "Which class is economical and will let me learn at an easy pace?". Furthermore, the book will aid the novice in first deciding what he wants to do, then finding the most cost-effective method. Queries such as: "It's not a straight-shaft is it?," or "Is it an LTO or is it straight-up?," or "Dirt or asphalt?," or "Is it a two or four-stroke?" will set the reader aside from other beginners who do not know what to ask, and who may end-up buying a chassis or engine they cannot race or resell in their area. Reading this book will help the novice separate the relevant information from the urban karting legends.

All karters have had to purchase at least some equipment in the very beginning. At the onset of their career, had they purchased the wrong chassis, entered a class well above their driving or tuning ability, some newcomers, at the time, such as Richie Hearn, PJ Jones, Scott Pruett or the Pedregon brothers, may not have evolved into the racers they are today.

Godspeed!

Jean S. Genibrel

Jean Genibrel

PROLOGUE
The Heyday of Karting

KARTING IS BORN

In 1956 Art Ingels was a craftsman and inventor who worked for Frank Kurtis building Indy Roadsters. At the shop Ingels had access to some salvaged tubing and hoards of West Bend two-stroke motors originally used on lawn mowers. Art, being the tinkerer he was, got the idea of assembling a little cart out of the tubing and the West Bends so he and the crew could motor around the pits at the races. A little midnight oil and some American ingenuity and the first go-cart was born. Art and wife Ruth took to the Rose Bowl parking lot in nearby Pasadena, California to test the little...well, whatever it was. The original idea was soon forgotten. The little tike was reaching speeds in excess of 30 miles per hour. Soon, Mr. Karting's wife wanted a putt-putt of her own. The competitive spirit overtook the Ingels' and the first race was won by ... an Ingels.

Spectators were gathering at the Rose Bowl parking lot at an ever growing rate to watch "those little things that go so fast". Friends and on-lookers were offered rides. It is not known if it was an inside pass or the ole' crossover maneuver that sparked the first "organized" race, but excitement grew and home-builts started showing up every Saturday at the old hang-out. Races were organized every weekend.

At the speeds they were reaching, the little 2.5 horse, two-stroke West Bends ("W.B.") were ideal, but racers being what they are, never going fast enough and all, started showing up with lower gear ratios, then another racer "shaved the head" to raise compression and increase power on his W.B., and the race was on in more than one way. Along with the faster speeds came an increase in noise level.

The nearby residents, however did not share the enthusiasm of the go-cart pioneers. And who could blame them? They had paid the astronomical sum of 12,000 dollars for a home with a view on the Rose Bowl and now they had to listen to this racket every weekend. The new racers were soon evicted from their first hangout; unceremoniously expelled from karting's first "kart track". They just moved down the road to another lot at the Sears, Roebuck and Co. in Pasadena, and then to another location, and another. The local law was developing a severe annoyance for "those hooligans who think they own every parking lot in town".

In those days entry forms included maps to alternate "tracks". The frequency of "evictions" forced the "organizers" to supply the "entrants" with alternate locations to the event in case the race was "red-flagged" by the local law. Some events were completed in the late hours and only after sneaking onto several parking lots.

Enough was enough. The sport was growing at a rate only witnessed by the Yo-Yo and Hoola-Hoop crazes. Karts were showing up at races all over the country. Some machines were works of art, while others were a disaster in the waiting. Something had to be done before someone got hurt. The Go Kart Club of America was formed in 1957 with efforts concentrated on defining rules and safety standards.

When the go-karters were booted off the East End Shopping Center parking lot in West Covina, California, some enterprising businessmen saw an opportunity to further the growth of their business and the fledgling sport of go-kart racing. The "Go Kart Company" composed of Roy Desbrow, Duffy Livingstone and Bill Rowles grasped the opportunity by building the first go-kart track in the world. The track was completed in December of 1958 in Azusa, California, just a few miles from Pasadena, where all the action had begun just two years prior.

More and more races were organized all over the country and the competition was getting stiffer by the day; the motors were being pushed to their limits and beyond. Reliability was becoming a factor, and other engine manufacturers seeing an emerging market jumped in the fray. The Clinton two-stroke engines met the same demise the West Bends did. The engines of those days were not built for racing. They were used on chain saws, lawn mowers and small scooters. The racers, in their never ending search for speed, removed the governors and turned the motors well beyond their intended limits. It was not *if* the engine was going to blow, but *when*. Some racers would show up at the races with three or four motors just to finish the event.

In Europe and England the Villier two-stroke was the power plant of choice for most karters. Importing a go-kart engine all the way from "across the Pond" was out of the question. The American chain saw manufacturer, McCulloch, seemed to make a powerplant with adequate power and reliability. Several go-karters tried the Mac with great success and classes were soon formed around the new 510. Of course some hot rodders of the period just had to soup-up their engines beyond their limits and the venerable 510 soon gained the nickname of "Mc Clunk".

In the days when some racing organizations did not allow women in the pits, Faye Pierson was making a name all over the globe for herself and her family business, Bug Karts. Pierson was setting lap records almost on every track she raced on. She set a lap record and placed second in the first National Championship. Faye won her class the next year and captured a first and a second place in the International Karting Championships in Europe. The "Lady Bug" was sought after by promoters for her presence at races all over North America.

The excitement also attracted the editors of several respected hot-rodding publications. Lynn Wineland, editor of *Rod & Custom*, brought one of the little racers to the office. In the parking-lot, writers, artists, photographers and secretaries congregated with baited breath. The air was filled with the aroma of freshly consumed castor and burnt rubber. A cacophony of squeals, rattles, and ratatatas entertained the lunch hour speed demons of the day. After the smoke settled, someone asked: "What are these things called anyway?". "Go-karts" someone said. "Pretty keen, hey?" The name was not bonafide yet, but many had amassed enough nickels and dimes from comments such as: "Boy, these little carts sure go" and "Look at that cart go" to coin the name and spelling of "go-kart".

Some of the "Hot Shoes" of the day included monikers such as: Hartman, Verlengiere (RLV), Burris (Burco clutches), Emmick, Pierson (K&P Bug Karts), Pittenger (Pitts), Miglizzi (L&T) and Patronite (Azusa Engineering); these drivers and entrepreneurs grew-up with the sport of karting and they still make a living in the industry. Bob and Frank Airheart developed the "disc brakes" for karting. The design became standard equipment on aircraft-carrier planes. The racing brothers' idea was soon swallowed up by "Big Detroit"... Other innovators like Tony Miglizzi took a hiatus from karting to develop the drag racing slider clutch used by most of the professional drag racing teams. Tony and son Lanny returned to karting in 1993 to develop the L&T kart clutches on the same principles the drag clutches were based. Other names endured through companies and products: Gil Horstman's clutches and a myriad of other products, the Patronites still own Azusa Engineering, Kurt and Mike Burris operate Burris Manufacturing, Rod and Art Verlengiere own RLV, and Ron and Linda Emmick carry on the family name, while Faye Pierson still heads K&P Manufacturing.

Go-karting would soon become an American staple and a family sport all over the world, teaching millions the rudiments of motor racing. The heyday of karting sprouted talents such as Jerry Titus, Troy Rutman, Phil Hill, Jim Rathman and Swede Savage. Mickey Rupp went on to build a small karting empire of his own. Mickey always believed that karters could race with the best of them. He proved his point in the 1965 Memorial Day Classic, nearly winning the event, only to get beat by some unknown rookie; some Italian kid named Mario, Mario something or other. Lake Speed won the World Championship in 1978, with Lynn Haddock wrenching. To this date Speed's victory remains the only World Karting Championship won by an American. Will you be next?

Chapter 1
KARTING TODAY
From the Ashes Rose a Phoenix

The go-carts of yore were essentially fun karts. As competition increased, the need for more speed and safety grew. The go-carts became the precision racing karts we know today: safe, nimble and fast. Costs and safety concerns gave birth to purpose-built tracks and facilities where families and friends can recreate while enjoying the outdoors.

Karting is a form of motorsport which is practiced worldwide, typically on purpose-built, short, tight, asphalt or concrete circuits and on larger road-race tracks principally used for full size race cars. In the U.S., karts are also raced on dirt and asphalt oval tracks.

KARTING AROUND THE WORLD

Following its inception on the parking lots of Pasadena, California, in 1956, the sport spread throughout the world in less than two years. There are about 100,000 karters in the U.S. and Canada, and nearly one million around the globe. Kart racing is now only practiced on purpose-built tracks designed with "safety first" in mind. It is illegal to drive karts on private properties, parking lots, alleys and public streets.

Most kart racing is sanctioned by clubs, and national and international organizations. In the U.S., karting is regulated by the International Kart Federation (IKF), Karters of America Racing Triad (KART) and the World Karting Association (WKA). Canadian karting is governed by the ASN Canada FIA. In all other countries, karting is regulated by the Commission Internationale de Karting/Federation Internationale de l'Automobile (CIK/FIA), based in Switzerland.

The local clubs run under the umbrella of at least one of those organizations, or they at least follow the associations' rules and safety regulations. Many clubs also race under the insurance coverage of the associations. As a driver, or crew member you will be required to pay for a pit-pass, which includes the insurance, each time you enter a race sanctioned by the organization.

In Europe, karting receives the utmost respect from the public, and the drivers are revered as the embodiment of the consummate racer. In Italy, France or Britain, a driver's chances of progressing to Formula 3, and later Formula 1, are almost nil if he has not participated in karting. A national, and certainly

From its humble beginnings in Pasadena, California, in 1956, the sport has grown into the most popular form of motor racing in the world. Karting has been the foundation for many professional drivers. Bruce Walls photo.

In the U.S., dirt track racing (Speedway) accounts for about fifty percent of the karting. Most of the karts run four-stroke engines. In dirt the karts usually use grooved tires which are made specifically for dirt racing. Speedway karting is most popular east of the Rockies and particularly in the South and Southeast. Dirt racing is growing rapidly in Canada. Phil Tanner photo.

a world karting championship almost guarantees a driver a seat with a professional team in a world class series.

THE KARTING DIVISIONS

The first question which faces the new karter is, which division of karting to compete in? Keep in mind the availability of tracks in your immediate area, classes, costs, and the driving and tuning skills necessary to make the experience pleasurable.

Karting in the U.S. is composed of three basic divisions: Sprint, Speedway dirt and pavement, and Road Racing. Canada is mainly represented by Sprint racing. All three divisions of karting use the same concept of a chassis without suspension, the chain drive, and in at least most of the classes which can be recommended to a neophyte, a single cylinder engine without a transmission.

Sprint Karting

Recognized as the epitome of kart racing, Sprint karting is the most common around the world, and it is what most people think of when the word "karting" is mentioned. "Sit-

Up" is practiced on short tracks, generally one quarter to three quarter miles in length. The tracks are asphalt or concrete. A typical Sprint race consists of two or three practice and tuning sessions, two or three heats of five to fifteen minutes, and generally the day is capped by a main event.

Sprint karting, much like the other divisions, is divided into classes based on age, engine type (two-or four-cycle), brand, modifications, and individual specifications such as a muffler, or certain type or size of carburetor, and a weight minimum of the driver and kart. In addition, some clubs run "local options" such as a tire rule (which consists of a hard tire compound to prevent rapid wear). For example, a class could be for drivers over 18 years of age, running a Yamaha KT100 under "stock rules", with a "Can" muffler and spec tire, at 350 pounds minimum. All Sprint classes run on slick tires except under rainy conditions.

American and Canadian karting is gaining the respect and recognition it deserves from the world community. Many American drivers are making the jump from karting to full-size cars. Patrick Long, seen in this photo, drives for CRG.

Oval Track

Kart oval track racing is very important in the U.S.. Speedway is most prevalent east of the Rockies, with the South and Southeast as the hotbed of dirt karting. Dirt tracks are composed of clay, sand, or cinder. Most dirt ovals are 1/10th to 1/4 mile in length, although some clubs may run on 1/2 mile tracks. The surfaces are watered and groomed before the events begin in order to reduce the dust and to provide adequate traction. Most dirt tires are treaded and grooved to allow the treads to sink into the track to provide traction. Many tracks are going to the "slicks only" rule.

Oval track racing favors "offset chassis" because of the left-turns only encountered in that form of racing. These specially built karts allow more weight on the left side to improve traction. Asphalt oval karting most particu-

Sprint karting is the most heavily practiced form of karting in the world. Sprint is also called "Sit-Up" after the upright sitting position assumed by the drivers. Most Indy Car and Formula One drivers have their roots in Sprint.

rly benefits offset chassis. Although many a ovice has enjoyed Oval track karting with a straight-up" kart.

Dirt Oval karting has the honor of being he least expensive form of karting.

Enduro and Road Racing

Enduro, as the name implies, is a test of ndurance for the driver as well as the kart nd engine. These events are run on long ports-car road courses such as Mosport, Sears oint Raceway, Road America, Watkins Glen, Charlotte and Daytona. An Enduro can last 5 minutes to an hour. The speeds attained an reach 140 to 150 miles per hour due to he length of the tracks and the laid down

Enduro karting is still popular in certain areas. Enduro karting is mostly practiced by veterans who have been racing for a number of years. KART photo.

position of the driver, which lowers the cener of gravity and reduces the aerodynamic drag. An Enduro kart is easily recognized by ts low, long, sleek shape and the characteristic butterfly steering wheel. These karts are usually raced by experienced karters who have invested countless hours in development and testing. The engines used in those classes are for the most part highly sophisticated. Tuning and repairing Enduro engines may be quite frustrating to a newcomer who does not have the specialized knowledge and access to the parts.

Road Racing is a name mostly used for the "Sit-Ups" that run on the larger road courses. These karts are usually the same karts raced in Sprint racing. The "Shifters" form a large contingent in road racing.

Shifters

Most Sprint and Road Racing clubs, and the major associations, have classes for the "Shifters" (Gearbox Karts). Typically, the powerplants are modified water-cooled motocross engines. The major suppliers of engines to the Shifter classes are: Honda, Kawasaki, Suzuki, TM, Vortex and Yamaha,

with Rotax making a presence in the 250cc ranks. Classes are available for 60, 80, 125, and 250 cubic centimeter displacement engines and drivers from 10 years of age and up are allowed to participate. The 125 and 250 classes are primarily raced by older, well experienced karters, or new karters who have prior racing experience.

The 125 and 250cc engines are remarkably fast and many Champ Car (Indy Car) drivers keep in shape in the off season racing these machines. The Indy Car drivers believe that driving a Shifter Kart is the closest thing to driving a Formula Atlantic racer or Indy Car.

Shifters can easily be recognized by the water-cooling radiator on the left side of the kart, the gearshift lever on the right of the steering wheel and by the front brakes used by the 125 and 250cc karts. Gearbox Karts can reach speeds in excess of 120 miles per hour on tracks with long enough straights.

Several schools specialize in gearbox kart racing. These schools teach the peculiarities of Shifter karts, such as with the shifting, starting procedure and the subtleties of handling such great amounts of power. Many karters use their Shifter Karts for practice, and then move up to actual racing when they feel comfortable with their driving abilities.

PRACTICE KARTING AND ARRIVE-AND-DRIVE

Karting is also enjoyed by many as a form or noncompetitive recreation. These karters enjoy the sport without entering races. They simply go to a track on a non-race day, pay a small entry fee, sign the insurance waiver and they practice all day. Some karters practice with friends or family, and others do it alone. There is always someone at the track to chat with and form new friendships. Many drivers move up to racing with a club when they feel more confident about their driving and tuning skills.

Some schools, shops and tracks offer "Ar-

Sprint karts are very short wheelbase and the drivers sit upright. The bodywork is minimal, but the nose fairings are becoming very aerodynamic. Sprint karts run two- and four-cycle engines. Rock Island Grand Prix photo.

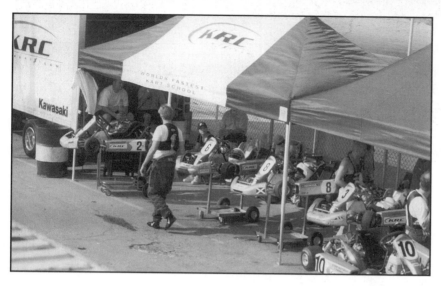

Arrive and Drive programs can be an attractive method of entering karting. Teams such as KRC in Glendale, California, prepare the karts, offer instructions to the drivers, and bring the karts to the track. A driver can compete for a whole season without having to work the kart.

Sun shades are used to protect the drivers, the crews, and their equipment from the elements. Karting does not require big tow trucks and trailers, so the pits are always open and safe.

rive and Drive" programs. The driver effectively rents the kart and sometimes a mechanic for the duration of the event. The driver can choose the events he wants to run, or some organizations have complete events the driver can participate in. If after a season of Arrive and Drive he decides not to continue in karting, he can simply walk away. On the other hand, a karter who has invested in the equipment would have to sell the equipment if he chooses to abandon karting.

Get references before embarking on an Arrive and Drive program, and choose a well established company with a strong track record. Keep in mind that in most Arrive and Drive programs, the driver is responsible for any damage to the kart.

Costs

Karting is the least expensive form of motorsport, bar none. A kart and competitive engine can be purchased for ten to twenty times less than a small open-wheel, or drag car.

A novice season in karting may include the cost of a piston and two or three sets of rings, a couple of sets of tires in a tire rule class, and a few gallons of gasoline. Even the karts

which run on methanol burn less than a gallon per race. Oil used in a season is less than a dozen quarts, compared to a case per race with a car.

The best way to keep costs low in the first year of karting is to enter a well represented class which allows few modifications, and one which enforces a tire rule.

VENUES

There are over 420 locations in the U.S. where karts can be raced. This includes some of the Super Speedways, which incorporate sports-car road courses in the infield on which karts can race, like Charlotte Motor Speedway where the World Championship tour stops each year in the fall. Other kart tracks are part of the infield of smaller ovals.

Of those 420 racing venues about half are dirt or asphalt ovals, and half are Sprint tracks. Many kart tracks maintain their own clubs, and some clubs maintain their own track. There are 175 clubs in the U.S., and 23 clubs and 27 tracks in Canada.

Some cities put on street kart races. The karts in this photo are racing at the Rock Island Grand Prix, in Illinois. The city fathers like the events because of the crowds they draw, and the karters get to race in front of thousands of spectators. The gate receipts and sponsors create the prize money. Photo courtesy Rock Island Grand Prix.

Sprint Karting Is the Epitome of Kart Racing

Chapter 2

KARTING AND YOU

"Karting is the ultimate form of motorsport" — Ayrton Senna

Novice karters usually have a multitude of questions about the sport: "How fast do they go?", "How do I get into this?", "How much does it cost?" Before those questions can be answered "they", "this" and "it" should be defined. The first questions for us to ask at this time are: "Exactly what is a kart?" and "What is karting?"

A KART DEFINED

Probably one of the most salient factors which define a kart is the fact that the vehicles do not have a suspension as is used on other race cars. A kart chassis is designed to flex and twist to act as the suspension to absorb the bumps on the track. The absence of suspension creates four major positive design benefits: 1—The driver can sit very low in the frame, thus lowering the center of gravity. This refines handling to a level only surpassed by the fastest of open-wheel race cars. 2—The overall package of driver, chassis and engine can make for a very light kart which reduces the need for larger or more numerous components such as with the brakes, clutch and tires. This attribute also makes the kart easy to store and to work on. 3—The freedom from suspension eliminates the need for a trans-

mission and rear axle. The utter simplicity of the chain drive simplifies changing gear ratios, and cuts gearing and lubricant costs to the bone. 4—The low weight and small chassis space available encourage the use of a small engine which simplifies and lessens the cost of tuning, repairs and maintenance.

KARTING DEFINED

Karting is a motorsport practiced on short, tight race tracks. In the U.S. (and at a few tracks in Canada), karting is often undertaken on dirt oval tracks. The small package required by karting calls for limited real-estate and other resources such as lighting and parking. The collection of these attributes described for karts and karting make the sport the least expensive form of motorsport in the world. In karting the sum of the benefits is greater than the parts to yield the greatest bang for the buck.

The Learning Curve

There is a learning curve in any sport. It would be foolish for someone who has never played golf to pick up a golf bag, walk on the links and expect to beat an opponent who has played even just a few rounds before. In

Karting has several divisions, classes, engines, and engine types to fit all needs, wants, and desires.

Kart chassis are easily identified by their full tubular construction, total lack of suspension, solid straight axle, and generally karts utilise brakes on the rear axle only. This basic, straightforward design allows simple steering, braking, power transmission, and rear axle designs. Courtesy Invader.

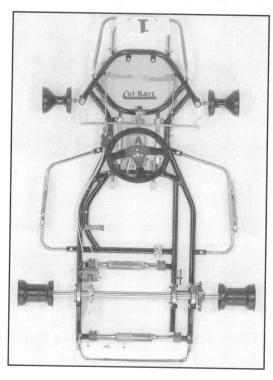

karting, the dilemma stems from the fact that most of the people who get into the sport already know how to *drive*. Unfortunately, they do not know how to *race*.

Learning how to race is just as time consuming as learning how to play golf, tennis or any other sport and it is a never ending process. Professional drivers in Indy Car say that they still learn something each and every race. The novice karter must give the learning curve some time to develop.

The karters who win the big races have been competing for many years; they have learned the basics of chassis and engine tuning and have developed their driving skills. Some of those basics can be learned from books, schools, other karters and shops. During the learning process the student must have the correct equipment and race in novice-friendly classes. Trying to learn karting with the wrong equipment, or in a too far advanced

This photo illustrates the simplicity of the kart chassis and drive train. Some classes run no clutch at all, and others dictate a low clutch engagement speed, yet allowing the engine to idle.

class can become a very stressful and disappointing experience.

Unfortunately, most of the karters who drop-out of the sport do so because they were unwilling to follow the learning curve and they got discouraged prematurely. The publisher of this book produces other self-help publications to assist karters from every ranks.

KARTING VERSUS OTHER FORMS OF MOTORSPORTS

Why is karting the ultimate form of motorsport? Simply put: cost, time and resources. In karting the equipment is relatively inexpensive, the technology is very basic and can be learned effortlessly if the novice reads and listens. Time: due to the low number and the simplicity of their components, karts are quick and easy to maintain and repair. Learning: karting, with its relative simplicity also offers an ideal medium to teach drivers to recognize the limits of adhesion without the inherent dangers attributed to full size race cars.

Karting requires very little working and storage space. Most karters use a single or double car garage for working on their machines and storing their equipment. Karts can be hung from ceilings or on walls for storage.

Many American and Canadian karters have progressed to lofty driving careers. Scott Pruett went on to win the Trans Am Championship. He and Richie Hearn, Alex Baron and Brian Herta now race Indy Cars. Philip Gibler is driving in Europe. Lake Speed of NASCAR fame was the first and only American world karting champion, and of course, Canadian Jacques Villeneuve went on to win the Formula One Championship in 1997.

There are other major features to karting over full size cars which are often overlooked. One is the space needed to work on the kart. A small garage or shed is sufficient to store and maintain a kart, while a full size car requires at the very least, a garage or small shop. Second is transportation. Towing a big car re-

Many karters have moved on to Indy and Trans Am cars. Karting is the best place to learn the basics of motor racing for the young and not-so-young drivers. Let your aspirations dictate your course of action when entering karting.

quires a truck and trailer, while a kart and gear can be taken to the track with a small pickup or van. Third, repairing a crashed car can be quite costly, time consuming and requires special tools and knowledge; a crashed kart can be repaired in much less time and with fewer resources.

The maintenance program of a kart, if you enter the classes recommended in this book, should not exceed a few hours a month.

Learning Made Easy

The simplicity of the chassis, the low number of moving parts in the engines used in karting, the simple braking systems and lack of drivetrain make karting the most simple form of motorsport to learn. The driver can concentrate on honing his driving skills instead of playing mechanic.

In the U.S. no racing license is needed and a physical exam is not mandatory, although it is recommended to have a doctor check you out, especially if you are over 40. Canadian clubs require a license, but those are easily

Karting also has races on dirt and has been the foundation for many a pro race car driver. Speedway karting is very popular primarily east of the Rockies and in the Southern States. The sport is growing quickly in Canada.

obtained. A licensing program teaches the basics of racing such as the flags, driving courtesy, passing procedures, etc.

CHILDREN AND KART RACING

There is no doubt that as a prerequisite to a racing career, karting is the epitome of the ideal mentor. The tracks are designed in such

It is never too early to teach kids the basics of safe, responsible driving and friendly competition. Karting classes start at five years of age, and of course boys and girls are welcome.

a way that the karts can be pushed to the limits without the risk of coming in contact with a non-movable object. In a spin, the light weight of the kart allows the driver to recover quickly and safely, usually without any damage. This allows the karter to safely learn the limits of a race car without the inherent dangers and fears present in auto racing. This is the type of skills that can only be learned in karting.

Karting can be entered as early as the age of five (5). By the time a youngster reaches 16 he has already acquired the experience and the conditioning of a veteran driver. Karting teaches many driving skills and disciplines which, when learned at a young age, will carry through a lifetime of good driving habits. The root values of self discipline acquired by a youngster in karting will erect the base for a lifetime of positive achievements.

Preparing Children for Karting

WKA and some clubs have "Baby Kart" classes where the beginning age is five (5). The basic tenet of dealing with a child this young and racing, is to know if he wants to race. If the youngster does not like the sport he will not enjoy it. Handle the initiation the same as you would for yourself as an adult karting novice. Take the child to a race or practice session. Have him or her sit in a kart and see how it feels to be behind the wheel. A Cadet or Baby Kart may look small to an adult, but it can be intimidating to a youngster who may not even know which pedal is the brake.

Remember that children cannot be talked into doing something they do not want to do.

A little practice working the pedals and the steering with the engine off, and a young driver can be ready for his first laps. When the engine is started the driver must wear all the safety equipment and drive on approved properties. In this photo the engine is off and the instructor is explaining the use of the pedals and steering to the youngster.

If they get involved in a sport they enjoy, they will do well. The key to success as a parent with a child in racing, is to let him grow at his own pace.

Parents can rent a kart from a shop or school and take their youngster to a practice day. There, the new driver can be taught the basics of braking, accelerating and turning. Remember that contrary to adults, younger drivers do not know even the most basic rudiments of operating an automobile. If, after the school or the practice session, the young driver likes karting, the parents can then make arrangements to purchase the equipment.

GETTING INVOLVED

Like any journey, a trip into the sport of karting starts with the first step; but before taking that first step, it is good to map the road ahead. Now that you know what karting is and what its features are, it is time to determine what type of karting you prefer, and which is right for you. Go to a kart shop and to a track. See the racing in person. Perhaps dirt oval is your cup of tea or Sprint may have a stronger appeal—only you can tell.

Points to Ponder

- Consider the age of the person you are looking at karting for.
- Physical condition and conditioning also require reflection.
- Marital status and age of children.
- Financial situation.
- Time available to travel.
- Space to work on the kart.
- Transportation available to get to the track.
- What hobbies do you currently have?
- Have you been involved in other forms of motorsports in the past?
- How long have you wanted to race?

Points To Consider

- Who are you looking at karting for? Yourself, child, spouse?
- Do you prefer road type racing, or Oval track?
- If Oval track, do you prefer dirt or asphalt?
- Do you prefer two or four-cycle engines?
- Type of kart you need: Cadet, Enduro, Sprint, Oval asphalt or dirt, Shifter?
- Club and Association to join.
- Class you want to race in.
- Do you want to buy new or used?
- Accessories and tools you will need.

Young executives find karting a very relaxing form of entertainment and an ideal way to sharpen the competitive edge for Monday morning meetings back at the Ivory Tower. The driver in this photo is 6 feet 2 inches tall and well over 220 pounds; he is still very competitive in his class.

When young drivers grow up they will have learned one of the most important arts in motorsports: communication. Here Canadian karting champion "Smokin" Steve Pickering discusses race setups with the crew chief.

Chapter 3

TWO AND FOUR-CYCLES
Different Strokes for Different Folks

Following the format of this book, you should have first chosen the division (Sprint, Oval dirt or asphalt, or Road Race) you wish to enter and you should have determined the distances you are willing to travel to race. You should also have visited a track within your allocated driving distance. Now choose a type of powerplant.

THE FOUR-STROKES

The four-cycle (four-stroke) engine was originally designed by Nikolaus Otto in 1876. This construction consists of a piston moving in a closed cylinder and a pair of valves; one to take in the air/fuel mixture and another to expel the burnt gases after combustion is complete. The process is closely timed to produce four separate strokes, or functional cycles: Intake, Compression, Power, and Exhaust.

The four-stroke engines in karting come in two forms: The "flat-head" design as used by Briggs & Stratton and Tecumseh, and the "overhead valve" design as used by Honda. The flat-heads have the valves and ports installed in the block. The overhead valve engines have their valves and ports installed in the cylinder head.

Four-Stroke Classes

In the U.S., the Briggs & Stratton five-horsepower engines constitute the bulk of the racing four-strokes in karting. To a lesser extent, the Tecumseh and Honda four-strokes are also raced, but their use is limited to specific geographical areas. The Honda classes are also good entry levels for novices in the Provinces as this powerplant is the most prevalent four-cycle there. When choosing a four-cycle engine, look at the stock classes as they are easier to tune, and with "stock" rules they are generally the least expensive to prepare and operate.

The Honda four-cycle is of the overhead valve type. This design is more modern, reduces pollution, and is more powerful than the flat-heads.

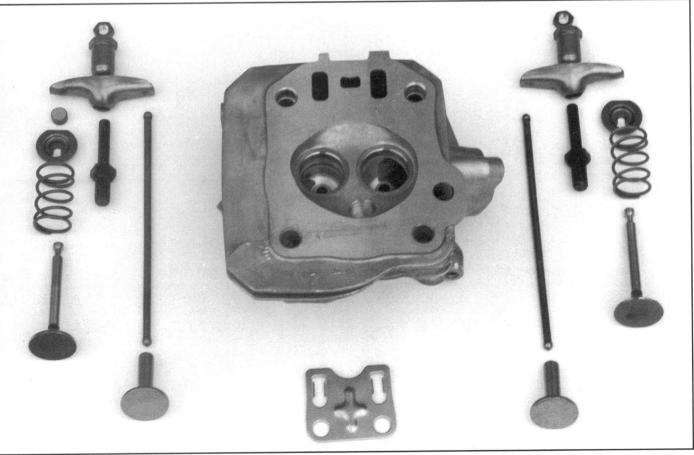

The exhaust system used on the four-cycles is usually composed of nothing more than a straight or curved pipe. Sometimes tracks will require a simple muffler.

The classes built around the four-cycle engines are based on age, weight and modifications. The karter should first study the rules of the class in which he is planning on racing. Do not wait to get to your first race to find out what class you can run, or if the engine is even legal at that track.

THE TWO-STROKES

It is generally accepted that the two-stroke engine was invented by Sir Dugald Clerk of England near the end of the 19th Century. The more sophisticated form of this engine using crankcase compression for the induction process, including the control of the timing and area of the exhaust, transfer and intake ports by the piston, was patented by Joseph Day in England in 1891.

Two-stroke (two-cycle) engines differ greatly from those found in passenger cars. Two-stroke engines do not have poppet valves, camshafts or pushrods. The name "two stroke" stems from the fact that these powerplants require one up stroke and one down stroke to complete a cycle. A complete cycle consists of Intake and Compression, and Ignition and Exhaust.

Two-strokes use ports and windows in their cylinder to allow the gases to enter and exit the combustion area. The piston acts as the valves of a four-cycle engine, opening and closing the ports at precisely timed intervals to allow the gases to enter and exit the cylinder (see diagram).

Two-Stroke Classes

The two-stroke classes are broken down by engine manufacturers, age of the drivers and the type of exhaust used. In the U.S. and Canada, the most learner-friendly two-stroke classes are composed primarily of the Yamaha KT-100 engine with a "Box" muffler, the HPVs and where available, the US820. The mufflers keep the RPM lower than if equipped with an expansion chamber and the fixed design prohibits the karters from making adjustments or modifications. This concept evens-out the competition, keeps costs down and improves reliability. Many clubs run a tire rule with the Box classes to further reduce costs and tighten-up competition.

There are two Box classes: Box, using the

The two-cycles and some of the four-cycles require an external gas tank. The Comers, Honda (four-stroke), and Briggs come with their own gas tank. Tanks are available in aluminum and plastic.

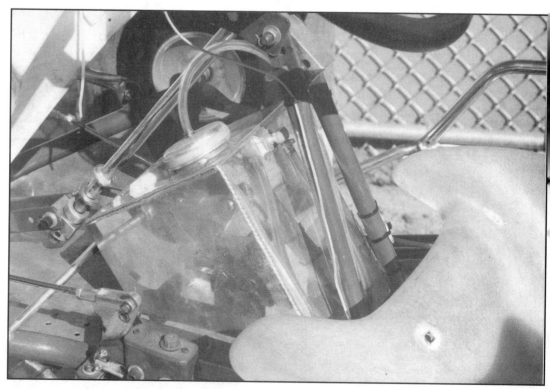

INTAKE STROKE. With the exhaust valve closed and the intake valve open, the piston goes down, creating a vacuum in the cylinder which draws the air/fuel mixture into the space above the piston.

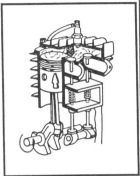

COMPRESSION STROKE. The intake valve closes and the piston moves upward, compressing the air/fuel mixture into the small space between the top of the piston and the cylinder head.

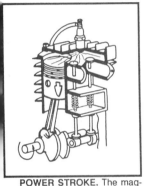

POWER STROKE. The magneto sends a high tension current to the spark plug, igniting the compressed mixture. The explosion expands the gases and pushes the piston down.

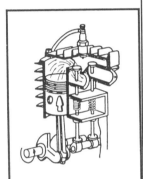

EXHAUST STROKE. The exhaust valve opens and the upward stroke of the piston forces all of the burnt gases out of the cylinder, completing the power cycle.

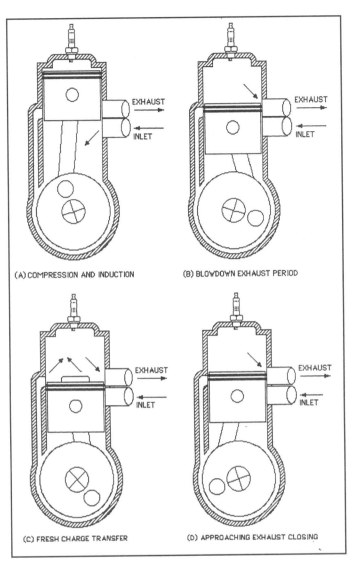

(A) COMPRESSION AND INDUCTION

(B) BLOWDOWN EXHAUST PERIOD

(C) FRESH CHARGE TRANSFER

(D) APPROACHING EXHAUST CLOSING

Typical Four-Stroke Engine

A — Intake Stroke: With the exhaust valve closed and the intake valve open, the piston lowers creating a low pressure in the cylinder, which allows air pressure to push the air/fuel mixture into the space above the piston.

B — Compression Stroke: The intake valve closes and the piston moves upward, compressing the charge into the space between the top of the piston and the cylinder head.

C — Power Stroke: The ignition fires the spark plug, igniting the compressed mixture. The heat from the explosion causes the gases to expand and pushes the piston down.

D — Exhaust Stroke: The exhaust valve opens and the pressure still present in the cylinder forces the burnt gases out of the cylinder.

Typical Two-Stroke Engine

A: As the engine compresses the charge, the piston skirt rises past the inlet track. This opens the way for the charge to enter the crankcase.

B: The spark plug has fired and the expansion from the heat of the explosion pushed the piston down the cylinder. During the down stroke (blowdown) the piston skirt closes the intake port, and the piston crown unmasks the exhaust port, allowing the burnt gases to escape.

C: The transfer intake ports are opened and the piston top allows the compressed charge to enter the barrel. For a period of time the intake and exhaust ports are open simultaneously.

D: In the up stroke, the piston and cylinder pressure continue to push burnt gases out the exhaust and the piston top closes the intake transfer ports. In the diagram the piston has closed the transfer port and is approaching exhaust closing.

Whether you choose a two- or four-stroke engine, find a class that is suited for the beginner, well-represented near your home, and in a division of karting you prefer.

Expansion chambers are still used in some two-cycle classes. These categories are better suited to the experienced karter and they are more tuning intensive, and since the expansion chambers allow the engines to turn at a higher RPM, the upkeep will be greater.

Four-strokes run their chain on the inside of the kart. All the chassis, especially the imported chassis, will not accommodate such a design. Look closely at your frame before deciding on your engine.

RLV YBX muffler and Super Box which runs RLV's SSX units, with the latter being somewhat faster than the former. These classes are in turn broken down into age and weight groups. The two-stroke engines for the younger drivers are controlled by a .600-inch carburetor restrictor plate for Junior I, and an .850-inch restrictor plate for Junior II and the RLV YBX Box. Classes are open to youngsters from eight (8) to sixteen (16), and other classes are open to older drivers. There is also a Masters class for those 40 and over.

Some clubs and WKA run "Kids' Kart" classes for youngsters of five (5) to seven (7) years of age. These classes run the DAP 50cc engine with a restrictor, and the clubs typically specify a gear and a tire compound to improve safety. The races are run for exhibition only where no points are awarded. The concept is widely embraced so the youngsters can learn the driving skills without the pressure of competition.

The gearbox class engines are two-cycle water cooled engines. These powerplants range from 60 cubic centimeters up to 250ccs. They will be covered in greater detail later in the next chapter.

BLUEPRINTING

Blueprinting is the process by which a race engine is modified to gain maximum power and to improve reliability within the guidelines of the rules. The rules allow some blueprinting in the stock classes. In both the two- and four-cycle stock classes, the compression can be increased. In the four-stroke classes, the camshaft can be replaced with an aftermarket one of set specifications, the carburetor can be bored, and the jets can be drilled to allow methanol to be run. In the two-cycle classes, the barrels can be relocated and the pistons can be cut down to improve port timing. The rules limit the type and the amount of work which can be done, but the power increase from the modifications is substantial. This work is not absolutely neces-

The two-stroke head on the left and four-stroke flathead on the right do not contain any valves. This simplifies operation, rebuilding, and modifying.

sary for a newcomer.

For the first few races, the new karter would be better off to race the engine as it came when it was purchased. Unless the engine is in drastic need of rebuilding, the new karter can run it without the added cost of a blueprint job. A freshly blueprinted unit is worth considerably more than a stock one.

Some local clubs and tracks may run rules and classes different from the ones published by the major associations. However IKF, KART and WKA regulations are customarily used as at least the cornerstone for local rules in the U.S. and Canada. Once again, it is vital to point to the assistance the local kart shops and engine builders can provide in determining which modifications are appropriate for your class and necessary for a novice.

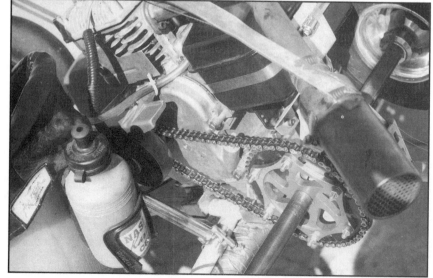

Chapter 4
ENGINES
Speed Costs Money — How Fast Do You Want to Go?

cquaint yourself with the engines raced in our area and choose one appropriate to your esires and local preferences.

A novice should find an engine that has a ride following and ample parts supply. Since he heyday of karting, several karting owerplants and manufacturers have emerged in the U.S. and Canada. Some engines are no longer represented by a dealer network or an importer. Others are scarce and raced by few. These engines are typically more sophisticated, very high-revving, temperamental, more difficult to tune, maintain and obtain parts for, and raced in small classes composed of well-experienced karters. Some of these units are used by pro or semi-pro teams who

When buying a used kart, try to find out who maintained the engine. Try to find a shop that deals with both two- and four-strokes. The staff will be able to explain the features of both forms of karting.

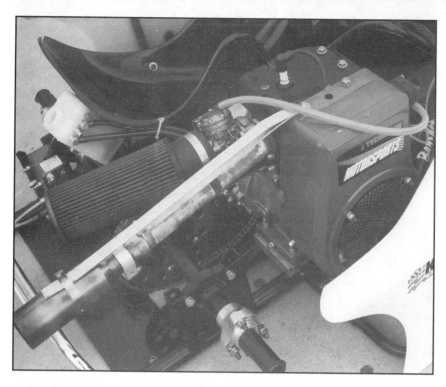

Tecumsehs are good starter engines, but they are not raced as widely as the Briggs. Check class availability in your area before deciding.

The Briggs and Tecumseh engines can be hand started. The pull starters are easy and inexpensive to use. Many karters remove these units in favor of an external electric starter.

youngster's powerplant, the DAP (Comer 50cc is also a two-stroke. Take your pick.

The Briggs & Stratton

For the beginner, the Briggs & Stratton 4 cycle single cylinder engine is one of the most cost effective kart racing engines. Briggs & Stratton is one of the world's largest manufacturers of industrial engines. The huge volume generated by the company has kept the parts very affordable for the racers, and Briggs' racing involvement has helped improve the quality of its parts and engines.

The company's commitment to motorsports is serious and its dealer network is very extensive. The engines form the base for many of the classes suitable to the novice karter. Because of the widespread use of the Briggs, the novice racing in a stock class will always have the option of selling his engine, or building it for a faster class.

The classes the Briggs can be run in are composed of the "stock" classes, the "stock appearing" classes and the "modified" classes. The stock class motors are the least expensive, the easiest to tune, and only require a minimum of maintenance and repair. The parts used are very nearly all stock, and they are easily obtainable from Briggs & Stratton Motorsports dealers. The few racing parts which need to be installed, such as the camshaft, are inexpensive and reliable.

are factory-supported and often very well financed. This level of competition is not recommended for a novice.

Different Engines For Different Karters

The most commonly raced engines in the U.S. are the Yamaha KT-100 two-cycle and the Briggs & Stratton Raptor four-cycle. The KT and Honda GX 4-cycle form the staple of Canadian karting. Horstman's HPV engine has become an excellent entry level package in the States, thanks to its low cost and simplicity of tuning.

In the United States, the Dap 50cc engine has taken hold in the Junior classes. The Tecumseh and US820 also have a loyal clientele, but their use is more regional. The Briggs, Tecumseh and Honda non-gearbox are four-stroke air cooled motors. The Yamaha, US820 and Horstman HPV are two-stroke air cooled engines. For parents choosing their

The latest Yamaha KT 100s can be identified by the number "787" cast on the right side between the lower and second fin.

The Yamaha KT100S

Introduced in 1976 in North America, the Yamaha KT100S is the best selling two-cycle kart racing engine in the world. The KT is primarily used in Sprint and Road Racing, but many Speedway karters have enjoyed years of success with it. The KT is an excellent beginner's engine because of its simplicity, low rougher surface of the older heads and the inscription "7ET" on the case bottom.

The old "straight-shaft" Yamaha is no longer competitive and replacement parts may be difficult to find. This engine is identified by its straight output shaft as compared to the taper carried by the newer models from the end of the threads to about the middle of the shaft.

Some Yamahas are equipped with reed or rotary valves. Reeds and Rotaries are the types of engines which are typically raced by the more experienced karters. These are often found on older chassis at bargain prices because the owner could not find a track with a

Comer/Dap produces a 50cc two-stroke which is quite popular in the Junior classes. These come equipped with their own gas tanks.

cost, broad class base, as well as its wide parts and builder availability in the U.S. and Canada.

To recognize the latest KT model, look between the bottom and second fin approximately in the center of the cylinder. The boss on the clutch side will have "787" cast into it and the boss on the ignition side (sparkplug wire side) will carry the symbol "Y3" or "Y4". The new motors can be identified by their cast heads which have a smooth finish, versus the

The HPV classes are growing rapidly in the U.S. and Canada. Some of the features of this powerplant can be observed in this photo. The fixed exhaust and clutch setting and the absence of need of a Third Bearing make this engine a prime candidate for starters.

Kart engines are attached to the frames via butterfly clamps. These allow easy adjustment of the chain.

class for his engine, or he got discouraged trying to keep it running.

A blueprinted late model KT100s can be sold easily if the karter decides to move to a faster class in a couple of years, once he has mastered the ropes in a more learner friendly class.

The HPV

The HPV (Horstman Piston Valve) classes are based on a four-part concept devised by Horstman Manufacturing to even out the competition and reduce costs to help new karters concentrate on their driving and apprenticeship, and to provide economical, competitive

The 60 and 80cc shifter classes can make a good entry-level class for some. This class does not allow front brakes and the clubs often run a tire rule. The lower power allows the new karter to concentrate on his driving.

clutch shield which acts as the Third Bearing.

The Horstman Piston Valve is raced in a three of the major associations in Junior an adult classes. The engines produce from seve (7) horsepower for the Kids' class, up to 1 horsepower for the senior class. The powe level on the HPVs is regulated by the size o the carburetors, and exhaust system allowe in each class.

The Gearbox Class Engines

The Gearbox classes are composed of th Honda, Kawasaki, TM and Yamaha 60, 80, 12 and 250cc water cooled motocross engines Manufacturers and associations dedicated t shifter karts, such as SKUSA, recommend th faster shifter classes to advanced karters o racers who have extensive racing experienc in high powered cars and who possess an un derstanding of kart setup, engine tuning and or have demonstrated safe control of karts fo a year or two in lesser power classes. Th larger displacement shifter karts are consid erably more expensive to purchase and oper ate. This is in part due to the front brake allowed on these machines, the engine cool ing system, shifting mechanism and gearbo of the motocross engines, and the frequen need to replace the tires. The 60 and 80cc classes are more learner- and user-friendly.

A shop can help you find the answers to fi

classes with parity for the established karters.

1. The engines must run with a specified exhaust system, which eliminates the need to test different pipes and "flex" dimensions to find the optimum setup for an engine.
2. The HPVs run a spec clutch (the EXPD-A) with a pre-set lock-up of 6,000 RPM. This feature allows the clutch to slip only while leaving the pits. The clutches on the HPVs require less work and far fewer rebuilds than those in other classes.
3. The wide power band of the HPVs makes for easy tuning and gearing.
4. The HPV engines come equipped with their own

Two-strokes typically require an external electric starter. An assistant is generally required to start the engine. What are dads for, anyway?

> ### Use the following guidelines and considerations in choosing an engine.
>
> ❑ Is the replacement parts cost of the engine you are contemplating acceptable?
> ❑ Are those engines raced on tracks within an reasonable driving distance?
> ❑ Are there builders in your area who can service the engine and supply parts?
> ❑ Is it a late model with a wide local following?
> ❑ How easy to tune is it? Consider the clutch, exhaust, carburetor and gearing.
> ❑ Look at the typical maximum RPM the engines turn in their class.
> ❑ Is the engine blueprinted, or is it stock? Does it need freshening?
> ❑ Look for value, not just price.
> ❑ Who built the engine, and who maintained it?
> ❑ Does the engine use metric or standard fasteners?
> ❑ A four-cycle does not require a fuel tank, third bearing support and its clutch and exhaust system are less expensive than two-cycles. Two-strokes generally require an air box.

our needs and preferences and to ensure you will buy an engine which can be raced inexpensively, easily and reliably.

By this juncture you should have decided the division, and engine type and brand you want to race or practice with. Note which engine and division you would like to race in on step three of the *checklist* in Chapter 12.

Costs

Staying within the stock classes, in either two-or four-cycle, will be the least expensive and most enjoyable experience for the new starter. Compare the cost of replacement parts, clutches and tires which can be used in the classes for the engine being considered. Even if an engine costs more than another, it can quickly pay for itself if it can be raced in a class with a tire rule. The stock classes do not demand clutches as sophisticated as in the faster classes. The lower power output in those classes reduces the wear, maintenance rates and costs. A stock class engine will also typically turn lower RPM and run cooler than the

motors in the more sophisticated classes. Lowered engine heat and speed are two very crucial elements in improving reliability and extending rebuild and maintenance frequencies.

Ask your kart shop about the maintenance that will be required on the engine you are considering. Ask what RPM level it generally turns; the higher the RPM, the greater the upkeep and repair costs. The RPM range can

Some engines used in karting are very fast and very high-revving. These are raced by pro or semi-pro teams. They form the vertex of karting and the novice should take a few seasons to learn the ropes before graduating to this level.

Value is buying something you need and want at a good price

Hondas are very popular in Canada. Their popularity is increasing in the U.S. The main feature of the Honda is its overhead valve design which improves torque at lower RPMs, and its integral fuel tank.

Engine and Class	Approximate Power	Approximate Peak RPM
Yamaha Box & F100	11	12,500 to 13,000
Yamaha Super Box	13	12,800 to 13,500
Yamaha Pipe, FY & F100	16-18	14,000 to 14,500
HPV (5 classes)	7, 11, 14, 14, 18	13,000 to 15,000
60 Shifter	16	13,000 to 13,500
80 Shifter	21-23	12,800 to 13,500
125 Shifter	40	12,000 to 13,000
250 Shifter	70	12,000 to 12,500
Formula A	26-29	18,500 to 19,000
Formula C	45	14,500 to 15,000
US820	11-12	6,500 to 6,600
Briggs Stock	8	6,000 to 6,200
Briggs Super Stock	10	7,200 to 7,400
Limited Modified	15	9,200 to 9,600
Tecumseh H-50	10-11	6,000 to 6,200
Tecumseh Star	19-20	5,900 to 6,100
Honda GX200	8	5,500 to 5,600

A typical beginner's setup. A stock Yamaha, with "Can" muffler. Note dry clutch and third bearing support.

be quite broad even with the same engine. For example, a highly modified Briggs can turn up to 9,000 RPM, while a stock-class engine will seldom see over 6,200 RPM. At this point, for a novice, speed is not as important as learning, practicing and honing the racing skills.

Consider the type of fasteners used. This will determine if metric or standard tools will be needed. The Briggs and Tecumseh are made in the U.S. and they use standard fasteners, while the Honda, HPV and Yamaha are equipped with metric fasteners.

Chapter 5
KART FRAMES
Different Strokes for Different Folks

Use this chapter to help you acquire a frame that will conform to the division of karting and the engine you chose.

In motorsports, evolution is a permanent fixture; a resident ghost haunting all forms of racing in constant search for improvements. Nevertheless, in karting, as well as all motor racing, evolution reigns over revolution. Of all the technology in karting, frame design has been the most influenced by progress and evolution in the last couple decades.

The American manufacturers have had to step up and match the refinements found on the European karts. The finish of accessories such as the spindles, master cylinders and hubs has now attained a work-of-art state in the imported karts as well as in the domestic frames. After all, karting was born in the U.S., and it is still as American as baseball and apple pie.

FRAMES

A kart frame (chassis) consists of three parts: 1—The front section which is primarily used to attach the front bumper, the pedals, the spindles and the steering lower support. 2—The center section is used for mounting the steering upper support, the seat, and master cylinder, and 3—The rear section houses the engine, axle and rear bumper. An oversimplification? Perhaps. But, simplicity

Modern kart frames have reached a pinnacle of sophistication. Note the wide track and short wheelbase for maneuverability. The finish is also very impressive. Most new chassis come bare without side pods, engine, tires and seat. If you buy new, order a seat according to your weight and hip size.

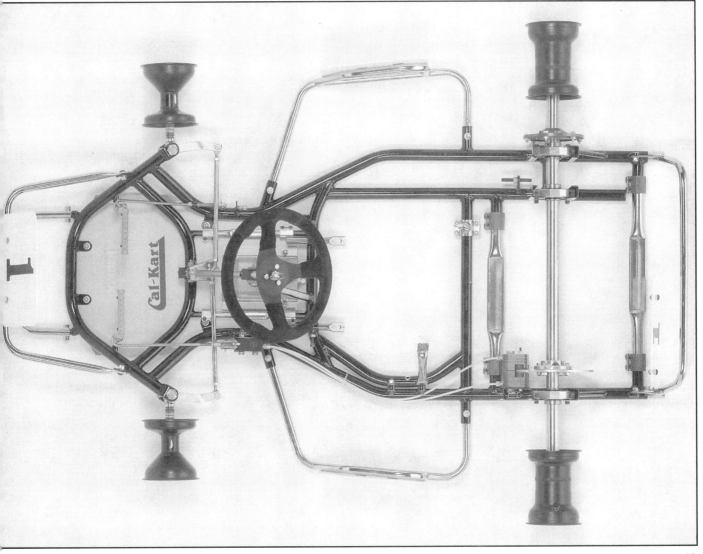

Offset chassis manufacturers also relocate the steering further to the left to increase weight on the left front wheel. Note the different length tie rods, and the pedal risers for young drivers.

is karting's middle name.

The chassis on a kart, primarily the center section, acts as the suspension and manufacturers build-in flex points to allow the chassis to "work". With age, the chassis can lose some of its resiliency and can take a "set", where the chassis can bend to a point of no return. In either condition, the chassis can usually be readjusted by raising or lowering the spindles.

Purpose Built Frames

There are frames for each form of karting and age group: Enduro, Sprint, Baby Karts, Cadet, Dirt, Dirt Offset and Shifter. The frame should be purchased to fit the division, engine and class in which it is intended to be used. The physique and age of the driver should also be considered.

The brand, age and model of a frame are not as important at this point as getting into something easy to adjust, inexpensive to operate, reliable, and with a strong dealer support in your area. Most importantly, get a kart that is made for the type of racing you are planning on doing. Think simple!

Spindle adjustments are quite handy to set the corner weights of the chassis. The setup on this Top Kart also features camber and caster adjusters.

Chassis at a Glance

❑ Sprint chassis are the most common in th U.S. and particularly in Canada. They a designed to race on asphalt tracks wit right and left turns. Most karts are buil around wheelbases of 42 to 48 inches an the driver sits up in an almost vertic stance. Many Sprint chassis include adjus ers called "blades". By turning the blade the driver can tune the chassis handlin Sprint karts generally use a round steerin wheel onto which the tachometer and e gine temperature gauges are mounted. B rules, the seats on Sprint karts cannot r cline as much as on the Enduro karts.

"Baby" karts come with mechanical brakes and small, solid axles. These karts are driven relative slow and they carry little weight. The frames on these karts are very reliable and they can be resol easily when the youngster grows up.*

❑ Baby Karts (Kids' Karts) are designed fc very young children. The age limits for th classes using these karts is generally fiv (5) to eight (8) years old. These karts ar very small and can only be used by driver of equally diminutive size.

❑ Cadet chassis are sized between the Bab and full-size Sprint kart formats. Thes chassis are built for the Junior classe where the drivers range in age from 8 t 11. Cadet chassis often come equipped wit mechanical brakes and a solid rear axle t lower the price of the package. Full siz karts are allowed in the Junior classes, bu typically, young drivers will be more com fortable in a smaller kart.

❑ Some Oval track chassis are very simila to the Sprint chassis and many oval trac drivers run a basic Sprint chassis on dir or asphalt oval tracks. For a beginner want ing to race Speedway, it is advisable t choose a purpose built chassis to learn th peculiarities of left turn only racing. Thes chassis are known as "Left Turn Only (LTO) or "Offsets". A "dirt kart" will usu ally have chassis adjustments ("weigh jackers") on the front spindles and the

Enduro chassis are becoming scarce as they are losing popularity over the Sprint karts. These chassis can be recognised by their long wheelbase and reclined seat. This photo also shows an expansion chamber as the exhaust on a Yamaha KT100.

Dirt karts often feature "weight jackers". These adjusters are accessed by the driver to change the handling of the chassis as the track conditions change during the day.

extend straight out to improve aerodynamics and reduce frontal area air drag.

European and American chassis vary primarily on their tubing size. The European manufacturers use 28, 30 and 32 millimeter tubes and American manufacturers use 1.25-inch material. By using different sizes of tubing the European chassis have a greater range of options to choose from, depending on the type of track, weather conditions and tire traction. Many domestic chassis have adjustments to tune the handling to satisfy the conditions.

The materials used on the European kart frames, is very similar to those used by American manufacturers who typically employ chrome-moly steel tubing for their frames. This material is very resilient and can take the twisting and bending demanded in kart racing.

The karts used on dirt tracks are somewhat different from the Sprint karts. A "dirt kart" will usually have chassis adjustments on at least one of the front spindles, and they often sport wings and side panels. Bodywork is more prevalent on dirt chassis to protect the kart

The seat position and chassis design of this Banshee oval chassis shows the extremes to which manufacturers go to increase inside weight and improve adjustability.

often sport wings and side panels. Bodywork is more prevalent on dirt karts to protect the kart and driver from the inevitable shower of mud and dirt in the first few laps of practice when the track is still wet. Used Offset chassis should be plentiful in areas where dirt track racing is more common place.

❏ Enduro chassis are easy to recognize by their extended length and wheelbase, butterfly steering wheel and low profile bodywork. These karts are designed for high speeds on courses with wide sweeping turns. The seat is laid down into a fully reclined position and the driver's legs can

When looking at a chassis make sure it can accept the type of engine you want to run. The rear cross bar (see arrow) of some chassis gets in the way of the chain with four-cycle engines because their chain runs inboard.

This Tony kart is equipped with a 50 millimeter axle. Note the vented and grooved brake rotor

solid. The latest domestic axles carry an out side diameter of 1 1/4-inch, and the Europe ans typically use 30 and 40 millimeter axle Tony Kart produces a 50 millimeter axl These sizes make good first time buys. Kid and Cadet karts often use solid axles, whic are acceptable.

The axle size is also important becaus several parts are attached to it: the brake ro

Dirt karts generally run single purpose tires with grooves to bite into the dirt. Many dirt tracks are going to slicks to save tire wear and expenses. This driver shows total confidence in his choice of tires.

Dirt karts generally run single purpose tires with grooves to bite into the dirt. Many dirt tracks are going to slicks to save tire wear and expenses. This driver shows total confidence in his choice of tires.

and driver from the inevitable shower of mud in the first few laps of practice when the track is still wet. Some European karts may not accept four-cycle engines on which the chain drive is located on the left, as most European karts use two-cycle motors with the chain drive located outboard of the chassis.

AXLES

The size of the axle can affect the value of a chassis, the availability of components and the handling of the kart. Older chassis used axles of 1 inch or 1 1/8-inch and some were

tor, sprocket and wheel hubs, and the bear ings. It may be difficult to locate some axle and their components if either is obsolete Furthermore, the newer axles are tuned t work with the chassis and the latest tires avail able; switching to a different size axle coul affect the handling.

MANUFACTURERS

The major manufacturers in the U.S. ar represented by: Bug/K&P, Buller, Coyote Eclipse, Emmick, Invader, Margay, MXK

Chassis dealers should keep an ample supply of karts and spare parts such as side pods, tires, steering components and axles. This spacious shop is occupied by JM Racing in Arcadia, California, the importer of Tony Karts.

hoenix, Phantom, Track Magic, Twister, and hite. The imported chassis in the U.S. and anada include: Biesse, Birel, CRG, Dino, nergy, Fullerton, Gold, Haase, Ital System, lly, KGB, Kosmic, MBA, Merlin, Parolin, ony, and Top Kart.

CRG chassis are available for Oval track, nd these chassis can accept four-cycle engines. Most imported chassis accept four-ycles. The domestic manufacturers offer hassis for both Sprint and Oval track racing. gain, the key to buying the right chassis is ot necessarily to buy the same chassis as the ne that won the track championship last ear, but to get the chassis that is right for ou. Local parts availability, ease of tuning nd adjusting, comfort, reliability, resale alue, and the specific use the chassis was

ome chassis come equipped with blade adjusters. hese are handy when going from track to track ith wide handling requirements. The newcomer to e sport can do without these devices.

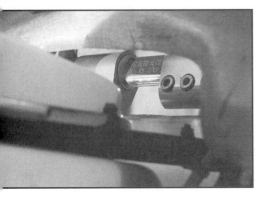

built for should be the major concerns for the novice when choosing a frame.

Use the following guidelines and considerations when choosing a chassis:

✓ How long has the manufacturer been in business?
✓ Are the parts available from other sources without going through the importer?
✓ Does the manufacturer or importer have a solid history?
✓ Do you fit comfortably in the seat and kart?
✓ Initial cost and price of replacement parts.
✓ Will the chassis fit in the division of karting you are planning on entering.
✓ Will the chassis accept the engine you are planning on running?

While a shop may not be able to answer all of these questions, it can help you find the answers to fit your needs and preferences.

NEW OR USED ?

Generally speaking, chassis over two years old may have lost some of their resiliency. Coincidentally, that is also the time when most karters replace their equipment. Two years also seems to be the limit for good resale value. Dirt karts are more forgiving in the longevity department as they are more adjustable and the loss in chassis integrity can be made-up easily with spindle and steering adjustments. A new chassis will have greater resale value when it is resold in a year or two. A used chassis will probably already be at least a year old, and by the time the novice is ready to move up to a faster, more competitive class,

Invader is one of the oldest kart chassis manufacturers in the world. The California company manufactures racing karts and "fun karts" such as this little jewel. Fun karts are not designed for racing and anyone purchasing one for competition is going to be very disappointed.

The correct seating position should include elbows bent near 90 degrees, slight bend of the knees and the seat angle should allow the head to rest comfortably. The feet should activate the brake and throttle pedals fully without stretching the ankles. The seat should fit slightly loose and away from the engine to allow some elbow room.

the kart will have lost much of its value.

When looking at a new, or near new chassis think about where the manufacturer and his dealers are located. Ask about the company and how long it has been in business, and most importantly buy the kart from a dealer of the manufacturer. In this case you will have a supply of parts and advice you could not get from some basement operation selling out its stock.

For your first purchase of a chassis, it would be advisable to find a less expensive one, of which you know the dealer and manufacturer as being well established, and who are nearby.

Of course, used chassis will usually be less expensive than new ones, but most American chassis are less expensive or about the same price new as a used imported kart.

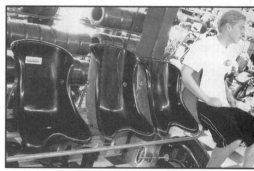

Try on a new seat and see how it feels after a few minutes. This karter had the right idea, and the shop was thoughtful enough to supply a range of samples to try on for size.

Think Simple!

In the beginning, karters showed up at races with the go-kart they had built in their garage and some engine they might have purchased at a surplus store. Soon, racers began to install two engines on their karts and others would hop-up their engines to a point where the stock ones never had a chance. The rule book was born. The Go Kart Club of America (now IKF) was formed in 1957 to set rules for karting in the U.S.

The first rules included classes based on the number of engines that powered the kart. Other classes were formed around the modifications that were performed to the engine(s). Later, the classes were also divided into engine types such as two- or four-cycle, and Junior classes were incorporated. Weight minimums were imposed to remove the advantage lighter drivers had over the "normal" population.

RULES

In the U.S., karting rules are set primarily by the three major karting associations: WKA, IKF and KART. The clubs typically use the Association rules. The rules are published in the Association magazines around the end of each year. KART only makes rule changes every two years.

A rule book is generally divided into six sections: General Rules, Sprint Racing, Road Racing, Gearbox, Speedway Dirt and Speedway Pavement. In Canada, ASN's rule book contains four sections: General Competition Regulations, General Technical Regulations, Two- and Four-Cycle Technical Regulations.

The rule books cover the Association operations, race procedures and duties, and the karts and engines for each division. The rule books also list the National classes with their respective weight limits, engines and their modification, and the fuel allowed.

The ASN publishes its own rules in the same format outlined earlier. The low number of classes and engines in the ASN makes for a small, concise booklet.

CLASSES

Today, the classes in Speedway and Sprint are very similar in IKF, KART and WKA. All are based on weight, age, engine type and modifications. Some of the weight limits may differ from one division to another or from Association to Association or even club to club. But, if a karter has a Briggs built to IKF or WKA rules, chances are that he can race

The Briggs & Stratton is the most actively-raced four-cycle in the U.S. Many independent organisations use the Raptor for their events such as the Hearn Competition Karting Six Hour Team Endurance Races. In this event the teams draw for the motors and race for six hours.

Typical classes courtesy IKF.

ahead) and cannot extend rearward past center line of front wheels. Side of front wheels and tires cannot be covered, must be exposed. Nose cannot cover drivers feet, i.e. feet and controls must be visible. Nose must be constructed of high-strength plastic or fiberglass and must be securely mounted to the kart.

May be mounted flush to bottom side of frame not to exceed further back than centerline of front axle.

401.9.2 Side panels: (See 105.2.13) Maximum height 14". Side panel cannot extend below main frame rails (rule 105.2.13 applies). Pods or panels may be a maximum of 1" per side wider than the rear wheels.

401.9.2.1 Side panels/pods (flat and 90 degree style) or FMK/FIA-style pods may be used. Must be securely mounted. Side panels and pods must be void of sharp edges. No metal panels or pods allowed.

401.9.2.2 90 degree panels may not cover any part of the driver's body. 14" maximum height (from the ground) all areas. Distance from seat to panel: 1" minimum, all areas. Minimum opening area forward of seat back to rearward edge of front tire is 22" minimum, measured with tires in straight ahead position. Panels may connect to nose piece.

401.9.2.3 If side panel extends rearward of the rear tires, parallel to front and rear tire, it must not extend past the rear bumper.

401.9.3 Steering Column Fairing: (See 105.2.4) Shall be no closer than 3" to steering wheel. Must have 1" minimum clearance between front fairing, nose piece, or side panels, and cannot connect to nose piece. 14" maximum width. Junior I can not run steering column fairing.

402 TWO-CYCLE SPEEDWAY NATIONAL CHAMPIONSHIP CLASSES

Class	Engine Type/Restrictions	Fuel	Weight	Age
1. ††JUNIOR I (Must be attained age of 8)	Yamaha KT100S/.600 Restrictor/ RLV Box Muffler, YBX/no Direct Drive/optional carb (see sect. 623.4.2)	Gas-Oil	235	8-11
2. ††JUNIOR II LIGHT	Yamaha KT100S/.850 Restrictor/ RLV Box Muffler, YBX/ no Direct Drive	Gas-Oil	275	12-15
3. ††JUNIOR II HEAVY	Yamaha KT100S/.850 Restrictor/ RLV Box Muffler, YBX/ no Direct Drive	Gas-Oil	300	12-15
4. ††SR. SPORTSMAN	Yamaha KT100S/RLV Box Muffler, YBX/Engine Clutch/no experts	Gas-Oil	350	16-up
5. †YAMAHA KT100S LTD.	Yamaha KT100S/Spec header and pipe/Engine Clutch/no remote carb adjusters/no experts	Gas-Oil	350	16-up
6. YAMAHA KT100S LIGHT	Yamaha KT100S	Gas-Oil	320	16-up
7. YAMAHA KT100S HEAVY	Yamaha KT100S	Gas-Oil	360	16-up
8. 100CC SUPER STK. LIGHT	Yamaha KT100S / 100cc Piston Port / 100cc Reed and Rotary	Gas-Oil	290 310 330	16-up
9. 100CC SUPER STK. HEAVY	Yamaha KT100S / 100cc Piston Port / 100cc Reed and Rotary	Gas-Oil	320 340 360	16-up

403 FOUR CYCLE SPEEDWAY NATIONAL CHAMPIONSHIP CLASSES

Class	Engine Type	Fuel	Weight	Age
1. JUNIOR I LIGHT (Must be attained age of 8)	5hp Briggs, .425" Restrictor/ no Direct Drive	Methanol	235	8-11
2. JUNIOR I HEAVY (Must be attained age of 8)	5hp Briggs, .425" Restrictor/ no Direct Drive	Methanol	260	8-11
3. JUNIOR II LIGHT	5hp Briggs, .500" Restrictor/ no Direct Drive	Methanol	285	12-15
4. JUNIOR II HEAVY	5hp Briggs, .500" Restrictor/ no Direct Drive	Methanol	310	12-15
5. STOCK LIGHT	5hp Briggs	Methanol	310	16-up
6. STOCK MEDIUM	5hp Briggs	Methanol	335	16-up
7. MASTERS (Must be attained age of 40)	5hp Briggs	Methanol	360	40-up
8. STOCK HEAVY	5hp Briggs	Methanol	360	16-up
9. SUPER STOCK	5hp Briggs w/Tillotson carb	Methanol	335	16-up
10. LTD. MODIFIED	As per Tech	Methanol	335	16-up
11. BRIGGS MODIFIED	As per Tech	Methanol	350	16-up
12. TECUMSEH STAR	Tecumseh Star	Methanol	370	16-up

Note: No axle mounted clutches allowed in any class.
Note: No water-cooled engines allowed in 4-cycle speedway classes.

404 IKF TWO-CYCLE SPEEDWAY GRAND NATIONAL SCHEDULE

404.1 Order of Classes
1. Group I - Junior I, Yamaha KT100S Light
2. Group II - Junior II Light, Sr. Sportsman, and Super Stock Heavy
3. Group III - Junior II Heavy, Yamaha KT100S Heavy, and Open
4. Group IV - Yamaha Ltd., Super Stock Light, and 200cc Stock

404.2 Official Schedule
1. Day 1 - Practice
2. Day 2 - Heats, Semi-Mains - Group I
3. Day 3 - Heats, Semi-Mains - Group II
4. Day 4 - Heats, Semi-Mains - Group III
5. Day 5 - Heats, Semi-Mains - Group IV

404.3 No Other Class(es) shall be run during the official Grand National schedule except approved Grand National classes, unless approved by the Board of Directors.

405 IKF FOUR-CYCLE SPEEDWAY GRAND NATIONAL SCHEDULE

405.1 ORDER OF CLASSES:
1. Group I - Junior I Light, Stock Light, Masters, Limited Modified
2. Group II - Briggs Mod., Junior II Light, Stock Medium, Junior I Hvy.
3. Group III - Jr. II Hvy., Tecumseh Star, Stock Hvy, Super Stk.

405.2 OFFICIAL SCHEDULE:
1. Day 1 - Practice
2. Day 2 - Heats, Semi-Mains, Mains - Group I
3. Day 3 - Heats, Semi-Mains, Mains - Group II
4. Day 4 - Heats, Semi-Mains, Mains - Group III

405.3 No Other Class(es) shall be run during the official Grand National schedule except approved Grand National classes, unless approved by the Board of Directors.

The three associations supply rule books to their members. These should be studied by the karters to avoid spending money unnecessarily and to remain legal and safe.

two-cycle classes. The ASN in Canada require the drivers to have attended a driving school to drive club races. This requirement is not a hindrance, but an advantage in that the drivers will be safer and more competitive when they enter their first race by having learned the flags, the basics of racing and the race procedures. American clubs and associations do not require any type of licensing.

Most of the classes that could be recommended to beginners are engine manufacturer specific where each engine runs in its own class. From there the classes are separated by engine modifications and restrictions.

Engine Modifications

The "stock" classes are allowed some modifications. These allowances are not intended to improve performance, but to ease engine building and facilitate purchasing of parts and to even-out the competition. At one time, the stock rules were very specific in that nothing at all could be done to the engines. In order to eliminate some of the manufacturing variances, the associations eventually allowed the engines and some of their components to be brought up to the maximum limits they had found on some of the parts.

The carburetors in both types of engine can be opened up to a maximum dimension. The cylinder bores have an upper limit. Some of the fuel and air passages in the carburetor can be enlarged. Other parts in the engine such as the crankshafts cannot be modified or altered.

In the Briggs stock classes, the camshaft can be replaced with one of specific timing. The rules also allow the head and block deck to be machined to increase compression. Limited grinding is allowed to the ports.

In the Yamaha classes, the three major specs which must be adhered to are the port heights, the piston skirt length and the combustion chamber volume. Practically no grind

Rules dictate which brand of engine can be used in most classes. This HPV will race against other HPVs. The rules in all classes require a chain-guard as seen in this photo.

his kart in any part of the U.S. A Yamaha built to IKF or WKA rules can be raced with most clubs in the U.S. and Canada.

Some classes run specific exhaust, carburetor or restrictor, clutches or combinations thereof, to limit RPM and clutch adjustments. The Junior classes, for example, enforce a restrictor rule, where a plate with a fixed-size orifice is installed between the carburetor and engine to limit engine and kart speed. Many classes also run on "spec" tires to limit wear and expenses.

In Canada, the classes consist of a Junior and Senior four- and two-cycle class, a Formula 125 class (Gearbox) and a Formula A and a Formula C which are direct drive classes using two-cycle engines. Canadian rules are very similar to American regulations in the

These karts belong in classes formed around highly modified rotary valve engines with direct drive. They are highly expensive and competitive.

ng is allowed on the ports. For more information on modifying kart engines, refer to the publications available on the subject from this publisher.

AGE GROUPS

In the States, the age limit in some clubs is as low as five (5) years old. These classes are for the Baby/Kid Karts which run on limited DAP engines. Most clubs also limit the gear ratio to keep the racing speeds safe. This class is for exhibition only, where everyone wins.

The youngest age at which a driver can compete in the junior classes in Canada and the U.S. is eight (8). Classes are available in

This youngster is enjoying the rewards of his efforts: a first-place trophy. Karting teaches young drivers responsibility, teamwork, confidence, courtesy, mechanical abilities, and, most importantly, karting is time spent with the whole family.

two- and four-cycle. The Junior I (Rookie Sportsman) class is open to drivers of 8 to 12 years of age, Junior II, 12 to 15. All the other classes are for drivers 16 and up. The faster Gearbox classes are open to drivers of 18 years old and up. A class is reserved for seniors of 40-plus.

Weight Groups

The classes in karting all over the world carry a weight minimum. In the U.S., if a driver is too heavy for a light class, he can race at a heavier level. The classes are broken down into "Light" and "Heavy". Generally, a driver of up to 175 pounds can make the Light classes which carry a weight minimum of 310 to 330 pounds combining driver and kart weights, depending on the division, engine or club. Heavier drivers can run the Heavy classes, which have a weight minimum of 340 to 360 pounds hinging on the association and division. The minimum class weights in the Junior classes typically range from 225 to 275 pounds combined weight, and they too can be divided by weight. Some clubs and associations run "Medium", and "Sumo" classes if the membership and attendance warrant it.

The weight of the Kids' Kart class as suggested by the associations is between 125 and 150 pounds. The Junior II Light class carries a weight minimum of 275 pounds and the Heavy class enforces a minimum of 300 pounds. Some divisions also have a Junior III class which uses a weight minimum of 300 pounds.

A few classes are engine specific, with a

This motley crew races the Junior HPV class. Win or lose they are always happier than pigs in a pile of mud. The sunglasses add the final touch to the intimidator look.

Senior, Heavy, and Sumo classes accommodate heavier and older drivers who would otherwise be hopelessly outclassed by younger, lighter drivers. These classes are often frequented by dads whose son or daughter runs one of the Junior classes. Statements such as, "Hey, Dad, watch turn three, it's getting slick!" can sometimes be overheard at the start of some of these races. Note how well this class is represented.

minimum weight of course. For example, IKF has one class for the Tecumseh Star engine and it carries a weight of 360 pounds.

The weight requirements may vary from club to club, between associations and depending on the division and type of engine used. As a beginner, do not be too concerned if you are a few pounds over the limit.

The Four-Cycle Classes

The Briggs & Stratton classes include: Stock, Controlled Stock, Super Stock, Limited Modi-

fied, Open and Modified. The stock Briggs in the U.S., and the Honda divisions in Canada make excellent places for novices to start. The engines used in these classes are easy to tune and quite inexpensive to purchase and operate. The four-cycle classes in the United States run almost entirely on methanol, which makes for much safer and cleaner racing than with gasoline. Canadian four-strokers are required to burn unleaded fuel only.

The Tecumseh classes include two classes, one for the 5-horsepower stock rules engine and the other for the stock rules 10-horse engine. The Tecumseh classes also run on methanol in the U.S..

The Junior classes follow the same rules as the Senior classes but the Junior engines must run a restrictor to limit the performance and reduce speeds and costs. Of course, the juniors run at a lower weight than the Seniors.

The Two-Cycle Classes

The great majority of classes in two-cycle karting use the Yamaha KT100S. The engine offers many advantages to the beginner and the more advanced karter alike. Other two-cycle classes include: Piston Port, 100cc Controlled Stock, HPV, the US820 engine, and 135 Controlled Engines. The US820 is popular in limited areas of the country. Some of the other classes are more complex than a novice may

The modified classes are well-represented in four-cycle. These classes are composed of seasoned karters, tuners, and engine builders. Many professional racers, like Richie Hearn and Scott Pruett, raced these classes.

Most tracks (dirt and asphalt), clubs, and organizations require the two-strokes to run an air intake silencer to reduce noise. This is not only the rule, but also a good idea, as they help the driver concentrate on their driving and reduce fatigue.

be comfortable with. Each of these classes are broken down into weight groups.

The HPV is also a good entry level class as the engines are very reliable and easy to tune. The HPVs are equipped with a Horstman clutch, the EXPD-A, which locks at 6,000 RPM to prevent it from slipping during the races. This feature eliminates one more element from the list of things to tune. The HPVs also must run a spec pipe. The gearing is easy to choose with an HPV because of the wide power band of the engine. The HPV and the Yamaha offer classes in the Junior and Senior ranks.

In Canada and in the U.S., these engines are generally required to burn gasoline. Two-stroke oil must be added for lubrication.

Most two-cycle classes are formed around the exhaust system used like this Can. This Yamaha is also equipped with a chain guard and third bearing. This setup can run in a variety of weight and age groups.

Gearbox Classes

Class	Weight	Age
Formula 60	280	10-13
Formula 80 JR	320	13-15
Formula 80 SR	360	16
Formula 125	385	16
Formula 125 Hvy	420	16
Formula 250	410	18

Front brakes are not permitted in the 60 and 80cc classes. This allows the karts to be used in other classes if so desired. Many clubs offer classes using these engines, with tire rules, which makes things very "newbie friendly".

Karting offers the most racing for the dollar (US or Canadian)

KARTING CLASS STRUCTURE

SPRINT

Tight asphalt road course type tracks

2-Cycle	4-Cycle	Gearbox
HPV[1]	Briggs[1]	60cc[2]
US820[1]	Honda[3]	80cc
DAP TS-40[1,2]	Tecumseh[1,3]	125cc[3]
Yahmaha KT100		

Age[4]
Weight[6]

ROAD RACING[5]

Full size Sports Car road courses

2-Cycle	Gearbox
Yamaha KT 100	125cc[3]

Age[4]
Weight[6]

SPEEDWAY[1]

Dirt or asphalt oval tracks

2-Cycle	4-Cycle
DAP TS-40[2]	Briggs
Yamaha KT100	Tecumseh[3]

Age[4]
Weight[6]

Chart includes the most active classes and engines.
Data may not conform to all the association classes and rules.
Tire rules may apply in some classes, clubs, and associations.
In the U.S. four-cycles run on methanol; in Canada they run on gasoline.

[1]U.S. Only
[2]Juniors Only
[3]Seniors Only
[4]Baby Karts: 5 to 8; Junior I: 8 to 12; Junior II: 12 to 15; Senior: 16 to 18
[5]No four-cycle in Road Racing
[6]All Classes carry a weight minimum

Chapter 7
CLUTCHES, LUBES, CHAINS
. . . And Much More

Clutches can represent a large portion of the investment the new karter can make in the sport. Study the subject and purchase a clutch appropriate to the type of karting and the class being entered.

CLUTCHES

Most classes of karting in the U.S. and many in Canada, use some type of centrifugal clutch. Using a clutch on racing karts offers many advantages. A clutch allows the engines to idle; the karts can be started externally, and it permits the driver to rejoin the race without stalling the engine if he spins out. When coming off a slow turn, the clutches slip to allow the engines to maintain maximum torque output. This process creates a great amount of heat. The karter must take great care to use a clutch appropriate to his application. If the clutch is too small for the engine/kart combination, the temperatures generated can cause the clutch to malfunction and ultimately fail.

Clutch Types

Karting clutches fall in two categories: dry and wet. The dry clutches are of an open and air-cooled design, while the wet clutches are enclosed and operate in a special high temperature oil. Clutches come in single, double, triple and four disc design, (Horstman and L&T) and certain clutches utilize steel shoes against a drum (Ratech).

Clutch life can be improved by using the proper clutch for the weight of the kart and the power of the engine. The heavy or high powered karts create a greater load on the clutches. These karts require clutches with a greater number of discs, and/or the wet type. In Sprint and Road Race, the high output engines and heavier kart packages use the two-, three-, and four-disc clutches. The single-disc (especially the air cooled) clutches, and the units with the single shoe mechanism are more appropriate to low power engines, lighter packages and in Speedway racing where the

These are the three types of clutches most commonly used in karting. On the left is a wet clutch which is manufactured by L&T; in the middle is a dry clutch from Horstman; and on the right is a unit manufacturer by Ratech. The Ratech clutches are used primarily on low-power four-strokes.

Smaller, dry, single-disc clutches require more care and tuning than the larger wet clutches. Double- or triple-disc, dry and primarily wet clutches are more forgiving than the lighter single disc units. A novice is better off with a slightly larger clutch so he can learn how to tune the unit without risking overheating it. Note the third bearing on this clutch.

Wet clutches such as the one in this photo are more forgiving than dry clutches. They cost about the same but they will require less maintenance than the dry units, and they can take more abuse in case the new karter accidentally over-slips his clutch.

clutch is only slipped at the start of the race.

The rules in some classes, like the HPV, require the clutch to be set at a very low engine speed. This allows the engine to be started without requiring a push and the clutch only slips when leaving the pits which saves considerable wear on the unit.

Other classes such as the "Direct Drives" use no clutch at all. The karts in these classes must be push-started. The classes these karts compose are highly competitive and generally frequented by the elite of karting. A drawback to these classes is that the engine will stall if the kart has to stop.

Karts should not be used to play on parking lots, as the slow, stop and go driving will cause a clutch (especially a single disc) to overheat and fail very quickly.

THIRD BEARINGS AND CLUTCH SHIELDS

With two-cycle engines, the rules dictate that the powerplants be equipped with a "Third Bearing", which is a support plate for the outside of the crankshaft on the clutch side. This mechanism reduces the vibrations and moment of inertia at the end of the crankshaft where the clutch adds to the momentum. The Third Bearing will increase the life of the crankshaft and the clutch.

The Horstman HPV is not required to run a conventional Third Bearing because of its

Four-cycles run the clutch inboard. Make sure there is enough room for adjustment and to prevent the seat from contacting the clutch. Notice how this racer has marked the clutch to indicate the number of teeth on the drive gear. It's no big deal, but it shows that he takes care of the small things.

The rules in the Horstman HPV classes require the clutch to be set at 6,000 RPM. This locks the clutch while the kart is on the track, but it allows the engine to be started externally, and the kart can resume the race if the driver spins out.

Lubricants are available from kart shops. Engine oil, alcohol lubricant, chain lube, and filter oil are all basic staples of karting. Red Line Oil manufactures a complete line of synthetic lubricants for karting and towing.

large diameter crankshaft, small clutch, and its relatively low engine speeds. This engine comes equipped with a chain guard which also acts as a Third Bearing.

FUELS AND LUBRICANTS

Two-cycle engines run a pre-mix, in which the oil is blended with the fuel. A specially-made measuring cup, the "Ratio Rite", is available for this purpose. Engine builders can recommend the proportion of oil to be added to the fuel. Mineral and synthetic lubricants are available for two-stroke kart engines.

The oils used in two-and four-strokes are vastly different in composition, they are used in different fashions and they are not interchangeable. With four-cycle engines, the oil must be added in the crankcase, much like one would in his passenger car.

The two-cycle classes are mainly powered by gasoline. Most karters use racing fuel as it is more consistent and lowers the chances of detonation. Racing fuel is also used because its chemical consistency facilitates inspection by the tech people. Consumer gasolines contain additives which can throw off the meters used to check the fuel.

Most four-stroke engines are run on methanol ("alcohol"). Methanol is safer than gasoline to handle, it burns cooler in the engine and it is nonpolluting. A purpose-made lubricant is often added to the methanol as its inherent lubricating properties are not as good as those of gasoline. Methanol costs more than gasoline and an engine setup for methanol consumes about twice as much fuel as one on

gasoline. Yet, a karter will be hard-pressed to burn more than a gallon of methanol per race.

As in other forms of racing, synthetic oils are becoming more dominant because of their greater protective and power producing qualities. Advances in technology have made possible some products available today, such as the alcohol fuel lubricant available from Red Line Synthetic Oil. This lubricant is perfectly compatible with alcohol because, like methanol, it too is a synthetic vegetable-derived product which blends perfectly with the fuel. The fuel lubricant does not improve power and it does not register in the tech tests.

CHAINS

The most commonly used chains in karting are the 219 and 35. The difference between the two chains is that the links in the 219 are spaced more closely than in the 35. The advantages of the 219 are that it allows the use of a smaller driving gear, and it is slightly lighter. The 219 seems to work better, and it is becoming the standard in karting. When purchasing a used kart with spares, make sure the gears, clutch drums and drivers, chain breaker and chain are of the same pitch.

Chain for karting comes mainly in the 35 and 219 styles. The 219 (smallest in photo) is preferred by the Sprint racers on both two- and four-cycles. The 35 is used more commonly in Speedway. The large chain is the 418, which is used on shifter karts.

Chapter 8
APPAREL AND SAFETY EQUIPMENT
Look Good, Feel Good

This chapter is a must read. Safety is the primary concern in karting. The safety equipment can help prevent serious injuries if it is purchased judiciously.

Karting is one of the safest forms of motorsport. Still, serious injuries can result from even a minor accident. In the case of safety, ignorance is not bliss! The new karter must be even more prepared for an accident than the experienced driver, because the possibility of losing control of the kart is greater during the learning period.

The newcomer should acquaint himself with the latest in safety equipment and apparel to purchase the correct pieces and prevent wasting money on a nonreturnable item which will not be approved at the track. While many kart shops will exchange some parts, items such as helmets and driving suits are not always returnable after they have been worn.

Protection from small injuries such as bumps, scrapes, burns and bruises is also critical. Smaller pieces of equipment like gloves, goggles, ear plugs, shoes and elbow pads require attention. Some of the safety equipment which is not mandatory, should be considered as necessary by the new karter.

The karting organizations have safety regulations, but the individual karter can use better equipment than what is prescribed by the rules and they can use the safety gear which is not mandatory. Before you can follow the rules, you must first know them. The IKF and WKA supply a very comprehensive set of rules which can be used as suggestions to follow if you are going "practice karting".

Kart shops are ideal places to purchase karting safety equipment. Kart shops have the knowledge necessary to help the beginning karter make the right decision about purchas-

Helmets are available from larger kart shops, such as Cal Kart of San Jose, California (shown in this photo). Choose a helmet from a large stock which offers a wide variety of styles and models to ensure proper fit and comfort. Helmets must conform to the rules of the organizations. The drivers can buy helmets which surpass the basic rules.

Alex Baron, ex-Tony Kart driver, has always been a safety-minded driver. He has vacated his kart seat for one in an Indy car.

ng equipment designed specifically for karting.

KARTING SAFETY REGULATIONS

Karting safety regulations are fairly standard across the U.S. and Canada, and most of the independent clubs generally follow the safety rules published by the IKF, WKA and KART. The organizing bodies have considerable experience in setting safety regulations; IKF for example, has been doing this for over forty years.

Under paragraph 105.1.1, IKF's rule book lists the following items which must be worn by the drivers while on the track: A helmet, face shield or goggles, gloves, jacket or full driving suit, high-top shoes and neck collar. Some of this equipment must meet certain specifications or certifications. Each division of karting also has its own set of specific safety regulations. Again, other items such as ear

Gloves with velcro straps, leather palms, and wrist protection. These should be a few of your favorite safety things.

Leather high-top shoes will provide some protection to the ankle. Choose shoes with a thick sole for comfort when walking around the pits.

plugs, rib protectors, elbow and knee pads may not be required, but their use can save the user from a lot of aches and pains.

NECK BRACES

Neck braces (also called neck collars, helmet supports or neck restraints) are designed to help reduce neck and collarbone injuries. In a spill, or just a swift tap from the rear, the weight of the helmet added to the weight of

A good neck brace can reduce the risk of broken clavicles and neck injuries. Neck collars are mandatory on all tracks and with all the Associations, and should also be worn when practicing.

the driver's head can generate enough momentum to cause severe whiplash and neck injuries. In a side impact or a roll-over, without a neck restraint, the lower edge of a full-face helmet is quite sharp and upon contact with the clavicle can break it. A neck protector will also be greatly appreciated when a rock, or in dirt racing a mud clog, hits the driver in the throat. In a flip, the neck brace can literally save one's neck.

Helmet supports should be stuffed with thick, dense, resilient material to absorb the momentum of the helmet. Preferably, buy a new neck support and make sure it contains thick, dense padding. Buying used neck collars is not recommended.

Karting neck braces come in two basic

Seating comfort is a large part of safety. If the driver is uncomfortable or if he cannot reach the controls comfortably, then he can easily make mistakes. Here the driver is so far back that his feet can barely reach the pedals and his arms are so extended that he will tire very quickly on the track.

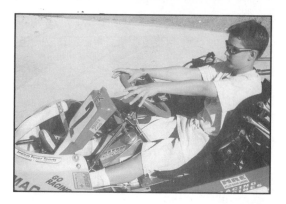

materials: nylon and polyester fabric. Both materials are washable in mild detergents once the foam filler has been removed. The collars should not be purchased used as they deteriorate and the foam loses its integrity.

Look for the following in a neck brace: 1– A good zipper and strong stitching. 2– The Velcro strap, which holds the brace in place, should be wide and long enough to allow easy installation and removal with gloves on. 3– Look for thick dense foam filler material. 4– Finally, check that it limits fore and aft, side-to-side movement, and that the brace is not so thick that it prevents head rotation. Some neck braces are tapered at the front to allow more comfortable positioning in any driving position.

HELMETS

The helmet is the most important part of the safety equipment gamut. When it comes to safety, there are minimum standards that are set by the ruling bodies, but the karters are allowed to use equipment which surpasses those standards if they wish. Do not skimp on safety equipment, especially the helmet!

Check that the helmet you are buying carries the latest Snell Foundation approval sticker. The Snell Foundation only tests and approves protective headgear. The Snell Foundation does not own the equipment necessary to test all types of helmets. So a helmet that is not Snell approved is not necessarily unsafe. On the other hand, a Snell-approved

helmet does not guarantee complete and absolute protection from head and neck injuries in an accident.

The availability of face shields is also a consideration. Some helmets are made for motocross or other forms of motor racing and they do not accept face shields. Also, if you

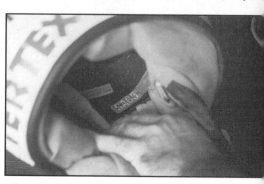

The Associations in the U.S. and Canada require the drivers' helmets to carry the Snell Foundation sticker. When purchasing a helmet, look for the latest Snell Foundation sticker date which is located under the soft padding of the helmet.

are going to run dirt, see to it that the helmet comes with "buttons" so you can install tear-offs. If you plan to wear goggles, or if you wear glasses, try them on with the helmet to see if they fit inside the eye opening of the helmet. Your kart shop can again be of service in advising on a helmet applicable to karting and in the latest requirements from the Associations.

Find a helmet which is not too tight nor too loose when you try it on in the kart shop. A loose fitting helmet can come off during an accident and, without adequate support, a helmet will not provide the safety and comfort it was designed for. At the track, your head will swell some (nothing intended here) from the heat, but the padding will compact itself after you have worn the piece a few times. Another hint is to keep the helmet on for 20 to 30 minutes when trying it on.

Helmets can carry an SA, or an M rating. SA stands for "Special Application" where the helmets are tested for three impacts, similar to hitting a roll cage three times. SA helmets have a fire retardant lining and chin strap, and their face shields are thicker. "M" rating is for motorcycle street use.

Helmets come in two major categories: open face and full face. The open face helmets do not offer enough protection for kart racing or practice. Full face helmets are used exclusively in karting. Again, buying the equipment from a kart shop will ensure you are getting the right equipment which will

Attending a good school can be worth a whole season of driving and the new driver will be introduced to the basics of safety and racing courtesy. Speed Zone driving school at Adams kart track in Riverside, California, offers a curriculum for drivers from age four and up.

go beyond the minimum rules. Most patterns are computerized to ensure consistency of sizes.

The correct fitting of the suit is also a safety feature. A loose fitting suit will be cooler and will allow easy, free breathing, preventing oxygen starvation to the brain.

When buying a suit from a kart shop, measure the driver at home first and take the dimensions to the shop. Many companies sell driving suits by mail order. Use the measuring instructions the companies supply to ensure proper fit.

Kart suits can also be ordered lined with fireproof material. While this is not required by the rules, it is a good idea.

SEATS

Seats may not appear to be a safety item, but the seat can be a source of aches and pains, bruised or even broken ribs. If the seat

The basics of karting safety equipment consists of an approved full-face helmet with visor or goggles, a good neck collar, driving jacket, gloves, long pants, and high-top shoes.

make your racing experience safer and more pleasurable.

Tips on Choosing a Helmet

- Choose a quality full face helmet.
- Try on a few different types of helmets.
- Choose a helmet which is on the snug side when new.
- Never buy a used helmet.
- Do not buy a child too large a helmet hoping he will grow into it.
- Buy a helmet with at least the latest Snell rating.
- Try on the goggles, face shield, and/or glasses if you wear any.
- Think comfort.

DRIVING SUITS

Most clubs and Associations require the drivers to wear at least an abrasion resistant jacket made of heavyweight leather, thick vinyl, or Nylon material, and full length pants. The Associations may modify or supplement this rule to require any additional piece of protective clothing deemed necessary. Driving suits offer far better protection than the jackets. Kart suit manufacturers have spent much time and effort in designing suits that

One-piece driving suits are safer than individual jacket and pants combination suits. Suit manufacturers can fit small and large drivers with custom embroidery and colors.

Several manufacturers offer custom suits. Drivers have the option of colors, graphics, and many add their name and their sponsors on the suit. Looks are important but safety should always be first.

Rib protection is not required by the Associations, but it is not disallowed. Many drivers appreciate the protection these devices offer to prevent sore ribs.

Remember:
Safety First!

is too small, it can restrict breathing and cause loss of concentration. Choose a seat that is loose enough to allow some movement, but tight enough to hold you in the seat while turning. Also, install the seat in such a way that it does not lean too far back, or too far forward; only the driver can be the judge of the seat angle by actually sitting in the kart and driving.

Seats with padding are not necessarily more comfortable than bare fiberglass seats. A good seat should have no bumps that could dig into the ribs after just a few laps. Uncomfortable seats lead to fatigue, particularly in Oval track racing, and fatigue leads to loss of concentration.

A wide rear bumper such as this one prevents karts from "frog-hopping" when tagged from the back. These are mandatory in Kids' classes.

Chapter 9
ACCESSORIES, TOOLS, SPARES

Karting is the most simple form of motorsport and karts are the easiest race cars to work on. Yet, some accessories, tools and spares are needed. Copy the lists in this book and take them to the kart shop and the hardware store. The new karter will find that everything listed hereunder will be the basics needed for his first few outings.

From the Kart Shop

- ❑ Battery charger
- ❑ Chain
- ❑ Chain breaker
- ❑ Chain oiler for dirt racing
- ❑ Clutch tools
- ❑ Cotter pins
- ❑ Duct tape
- ❑ Engine
- ❑ Fire extinguisher
- ❑ Fuel jug
- ❑ Funnel
- ❑ Gears

- ❑ Gloves
- ❑ Goggles
- ❑ Helmet
- ❑ Helmet and gear bag
- ❑ Jets (four-cycle)
- ❑ Kart
- ❑ Lead
- ❑ Neck collar
- ❑ Numbers and panels
- ❑ Ratio Rite (two-cycle)
- ❑ Rule book
- ❑ Shoes
- ❑ Spark plugs
- ❑ Stand
- ❑ Starter and battery
- ❑ Stopwatch
- ❑ Suit
- ❑ Tear offs (Speedway dirt)
- ❑ Throttle cable and stay
- ❑ Tires
- ❑ Tire pressure gauge
- ❑ Tie-straps

This tow rig is well thought-out. The van can be used during the week to haul groceries and for dad's work, and the trailer can be used to go racing on weekends.

An air tank and tire pressure gauge are two of the most important tools needed in karting. Of course, a simple tire pump will also fill the bill.

Chemicals and Lubricants

The kart shop probably carries most of these products. Several companies supply silicone gels, thread lockers and assembly lubes to the karting industry. K&N manufactures the filter cleaner and Red Line Oil has a complete line of lubricants and greases.

- ❑ Air filter cleaner and oil
- ❑ Alcohol fuel lubricant (methanol classes)
- ❑ Brake fluid
- ❑ Chain lube
- ❑ Clutch oil
- ❑ Epoxy putty
- ❑ Fuel
- ❑ Hand cleaner
- ❑ Motor oil
- ❑ Pre-mix
- ❑ Silicone gel
- ❑ Solvent cleaner
- ❑ Thread locker
- ❑ Wheel bearing grease

After you have determined the class you want to run, determine if lead ballast will be needed. Lead pieces can be purchased from kart shops.

Kart stands are not absolutely necessary when first starting out. But they come in handy when the pits are crowded and the trailer is up the hill. Choose one with large wheels, particularly if you race in the dirt.

These checklists are repeated in the back of the book for your convenience.

A Ratio Rite is an invaluable tool for the two-cycle driver. The cup is used to measure the amount of oil to be added to the fuel.

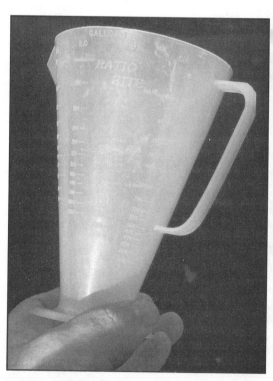

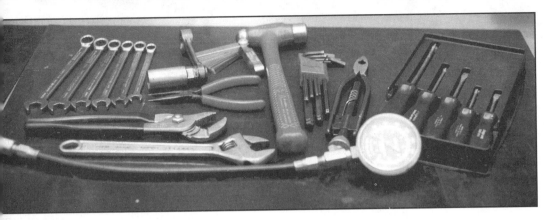

Basic hand tools the beginning karter will need. This tool set was all Standard as the owner raced an American-built chassis and engine.

Basic Tools

❏ Compression gauge
❏ Feeler gauges
❏ Plug wrench
❏ Spark plug feeler gauge
❏ Tire pump or air tank
❏ T-handled Allen wrenches (metric or U.S. depending on chassis and engine), snap ring pliers, screwdrivers, tape measure, wire cutters, needle nose pliers, pliers, files, hammer, hack saw and blades, extensions, small and a large adjustable wrenches. Box end/open end combination wrenches and socket set in either metric or standard.

TOW RIGS AND TRAILERS

For your first few outings you will not need much more than a small van or station wagon to take your equipment to the track. Later, you can invest in a small trailer or box van. If you do not plan on spending complete weekends away where your belongings would need to be locked, an open bed pickup truck would be sufficient.

Several companies manufacture small trailers purposely built for karters. These are ideal for those who want to travel in style. Small properly rated utility trailers are also up to the task. If you invest in a trailer, get one that

can be locked.

Do not try to transport your equipment in a vehicle not designed for the purpose. Overloaded vehicles can be dangerous, and the cargo may tear up the interior and vice versa.

Sun shades are always welcome on hot summer days or during those sudden Midwestern rain storms. These units are sturdy enough to sustain a California earthquake or an Indiana twister. Well, maybe a shaker.

Some chain breakers include the 219 chain pitch on one side and the 35 on the other. Invest in a good unit. The better chain breakers provide solid support to the side plates, and they can protect the chain from damage.

This box van carries three karts, a tool box, kart stands, chairs, a sun shade, a starter, fuel jugs, an ice chest, a pit bike, and even a work bench and vice.

Chapter 10
USED CHASSIS
Get What You Paid For

Before choosing a chassis, first decide what type of karting the driver prefers. Next, consider the price range. Buy what you can afford, but beware of cheap deals. Some karts are sold cheap because the importer has gone out of business and parts are no longer available. Others are simply old, or in poor condition. The best deal on used equipment is to buy the karts and engines from a team, a shop, manufacturer, or importer at the end of a season. The price may be higher than buying from a private party but you can get the history of the equipment and chances are the kart and engine have been meticulously maintained.

Consider the price of replacement parts. Compare the cost of a few parts such as brake pads, pedals, side bars, steering shaft, wheels, axle, and hubs compared to another manufacturer. The purchase price and the replacement cost of some parts on a used chassis may be greater than buying a new kart. Are the fasteners on the chassis metric or U.S. threads? All the imported chassis use metric threads; these fasteners may be difficult to find in some parts, and they necessitate metric

tools to install and remove.

A new kart will be easier to resell karting is the fastest growing form of motorsport. A new kart will hold less surprises than a used machine, which will help the newbie learn more quickly and with less frustration. Again, the bottom line is the financial aspect. American-built chassis are generally less expensive than most of the imports.

BUYING A USED CHASSIS

Most used chassis (especially Sprint chassis) will show some marks on the front hoop and side tubes, but avoid a kart with tubes worn flat or worn through. Most of all do not buy too cheap. In the long run you will save more money and enjoy the sport more by buying a good kart and engine.

Keep in mind that you are not looking for the next National Championship contender. Look for a safe, reliable and easy to tune kart that you can learn on, and a kart you can resell easily in a year or two if you choose. At least start the engine and sit in the kart to see if you fit comfortably. Oftentimes, shops will

Buying the wrong chassis left this guy crying in his beard. Fun karts are not made for racing. As such, these machines are not safe at the speeds race karts reach and they will not pass technical inspection.

"Let's see here. Late model chassis built for the type of karting I want to do; the track runs a tire rule and tires only have two races on them; no signs of damage; the seat fits and is in good shape; local driver; hmmmm. No gauge, though, but that driving suit is new and inexpensive. Let's do the math . . ."

ent out a used kart and allow the rental toward the price of the kart.

If you are buying from a private party, check with the local kart shop and see if they know the kart in question and its driver. Ask their opinion of the chassis and how it would work in the class and division you are contemplating.

Checking for Bent Chassis

The most important thing to check is if the chassis is bent. To do this, set the kart on a level floor, pick up the front of the chassis and note if both front wheels come off the ground at the same time. You can also turn the wheels from side to side with the kart empty and note if both front wheels come off the ground equally. Oval track karts will probably have some "wedge" dialed in. In this case the front wheels will come off the ground at different rates when the steering is turned side to side without a driver in place. A chassis with a slight bend can be reset by moving the

Pay particular attention to the rear axle assembly. Inspect the brake and gear hubs, the bearings and the cassettes. The wheel hubs can crack and strip. The axle could be bent or cracked, or it may be of an outdated dimension.

spindles up or down, if the spindles have enough adjustment available.

When to Buy

The best time of year to buy a used or new kart, or engine is at the end of the racing season. Many karters need the cash for the new season as they too are contemplating the purchase of a new chassis and/or engine. The shops may have a clearance sale or they may be selling their "house karts" which have been raced by their shop drivers during the year. Those karts are somewhat more pricey than the average run-of-the-mill kart, but you can get some really good starting setups with those karts and the buyer will know the history of the chassis and engine.

ACCESSORIES AND SPARES

When considering a kart, look at the accessories that come with it. The two most important "add-ons" are a tach/temperature gauge, and a starter. A new gauge or starter can cost several hundred dollars each; small things add up quickly. Consider things that may need to be replaced or rebuilt like the tach or the brake pads.

Does the kart come with spares such as tires, gears, engine, chain, brake pads, oil etc.? If you are going to be underweight for the class you are planning on running, some extra lead would be nice to get with the deal.

Sometimes karters sell all their equipment. You might be offered a sunshade, a trailer and a tow vehicle. Tools and shop equipment are sometimes also available. Do not get carried away, and know what you are getting.

Set the kart on as flat a surface as possible. Grab the front bumper and lift the front of the frame. Note if both wheels come off the ground at about the same time. If one wheel lags behind, the chassis may be bent. A small deviation can be adjusted with the spindles. Keep in mind that Oval track karts will probably have some "wedge" built in and the left front wheel will come off the ground first.

Instruments are very important in karting. For a novice a tach/temp gauge can be an invaluable tool to learn engine tuning. These units make a nice addition to a used kart.

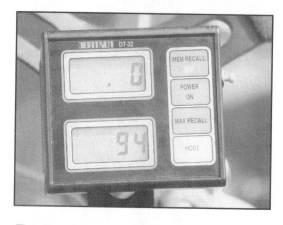

BUILD YOUR OWN?

" I want to buy the parts and build my own chassis" or "Do you have plans I can buy, so I can put a go-kart together?". The answer to these questions is very simple. Yes, there are plans available and there are ways to "build your own kart". However, the plans available are for fun karts which have no place on a race track. Should someone build his own chassis, the cost of the tubing, welding, bending and accessories such as the spindles, axles and wheels will invariably end up costing more than a good used imported kart, or a new American-built chassis.

Kart chassis have evolved dramatically in the last forty years. A home-built will not be competitive and the maintenance and setup will be more frustrating and this will distract from the learning experience. When all is said and done, the newcomer is better off waiting for another season than to buy a junker, or to build his own contraption.

Under any circumstance, never buy a home-built kart. Shade tree karts are typically not worth the effort, no matter how low the cost. The racing karts today are very sophisticated and trying to compete with them by building your own frame is usually a losing proposition.

WHERE TO FIND USED KARTS

A kart shop is always the best place to buy a new or used kart. The shop has a reputation to maintain and it would not sell you something you cannot use. Yet, "buyer beware" is still always a good motto to follow.

The Association magazines, club newsletters and tracks will often have listings for used equipment. Used karts are often displayed at races; there you can see the owner's operation and get an idea of how the kart was maintained. At the track it is easier to start the engine, and you might even get a few laps to try the thing out.

Some shops have a "rent-to-own" program where you can rent the equipment for one race and apply the rental to the price of the kart. At the very least, at a shop you can sit in the kart and have the staff help you find a comfortable seat.

Keep in mind that buying from a reputable shop can also buy some advice for the first races. Also, should you decide to sell the kart it will have a reputation in the area and you may be able to sell it for a good price. Kart shops are listed in the Yellow Pages under "Go-Karts".

WHAT TO CHECK

By now you should have decided which division of karting you want to race in: Sprint, Oval track dirt or asphalt. When looking at a chassis, the first consideration is based on the division you are going to race in. Second, is the age and size of the driver. For example, a dirt chassis will not do very well on a Sprint track, and a Sprint chassis may not have the adjustments and means of locating weight in advantageous locations for Oval racing. A junior driver will be more comfortable in a Junior chassis than a full-size or Baby Kart.

New equipment is usually the best approach. But, there are times when financial constraints, or other factors favor buying used.

This brake system was modified by the prior owner. The welding was of dubious quality and the plastic brake lines needed replacing. An "as manufactured" chassis is usually more reliable than something that has been chopped up.

New karters are better-off buying a used kart from a shop. The employees often know the background of the kart and they can recommend the accessories needed, provide after-sale support, and recommend setups for your track.

Even the untrained eye can spot the differences between an older chassis and a state-of-the-art model. The arrow points to bare metal which could indicate a crack in the making.

This chassis is also used, but it has been maintained meticulously. Note the stainless braided lines, welded seat struts, adjustable chassis, nylon bushing in the side pod supports, and vented brake rotor.

A karter may need some quick cash and may be willing to sell all his gear at a good price. In this case a slightly used package may be a better deal than a new kart. Package deals can sometimes include some diamonds in the rough, but beware as all that glitters is not gold. Again, look for value, not just a cheap deal and know what you are buying and who you are buying from.

1: Turn the kart on its rear bumper and look at the wear on the bottom of the frame. Some scratches and even gouges are normal as the frames set so close to the track surface that some dragging is inevitable. Beware of deep gouges and tubing "worn to the bone". Check for cracks and freshly rewelded joints. Inspect the welds at the steering supports. Now would also be a good time to look at the belly-pan to see if it is cracked.

2: Check the axle for bends by turning the rear wheels. A bent axle will not turn true or the wheels will turn out of round. Pull on the rear wheels to check for side play in the bearings.

3: Look at the general condition. Is the paint faded and scratched? This could be a sign of neglect or old age. Is the engine equipped with a brand-name filter like a K&N, or does it have an old sponge job that is falling apart?

4: Check the steering shaft to see if it is bent. A slight bend may not hurt anything but it could be a sign the kart has been in a severe accident and other things could be bent. See if the steering wheel is straight. Verify if the steering turns lock to lock without binding. Check the spindles for cracks and wear.

5: If the kart is equipped with a gauge, turn it on and see if it registers the ambient temperature. If it does not work it may just need a battery, it may need a cable, or it may need to be repaired or replaced. Check the tachometer when starting the engine.

6: Brakes: any leaks, pad wear, pedal feel, rotor cracked or warped? Are the brakes late model or are they old and outdated?

7: Inspect the bodywork for cracks, dents and tears. Look at the side-bars to see if they are bent. Look at the sidepods to see if they are damaged.

8: The seat should fit the driver without restricting breathing. Look for cracks and signs of wear on the bottom where it may have been rubbing on the track; some wear is almost inevitable, specially on asphalt tracks. Check the seat struts for cracks.

9: Start the engine and listen for any unusual noises. Observe the tachometer and temperature gauges. Ask the owner what brand of oil he used. Decals of quality products can indicate the owner took good care of the kart.

10: Is the chassis designed and setup for the type of

karting you want to do? You would not want an offset dirt chassis for Enduro or Sprint racing for example.

11: Preferably buy from a karter you know or has a reputation at the local track. Ask who built the motor and where the owner shops for his parts. Try to keep the same engine builder and kart shop.

12: Sit in the kart to check for proper fit. Tall and heavy drivers are often difficult to fit. Ensure that the kart or seat is not too small. Remember that there is some adjustment at the pedals, the steering column and the seat can easily be moved.

13: Do not buy a "no-name" chassis. Know who the manufacturer of the chassis was.

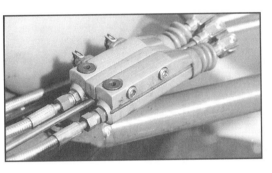

These master cylinders were clean and sported stainless covered brake lines. The dual master cylinder setup is more reliable, but more expensive.

14: Look for safety wire and cotter pins in the fasteners meeting that requirement. This will be an indication of when the kart was last raced and how well it was maintained.

15: Ask the local kart shop's opinion of the chassis being considered. Ask about price and availability of parts. Remember to continue patronizing the shop.

16: Stick with steel axles of a common size. Currently the domestic manufacturers use 1 1/4-inch tubing and most of the imported karts sport 40 millimeter axles.

17: Assume the tires will have to be discarded, unless the kart has spec tires. In such a case they may be useable for a few more races, depending on the compound of the rubber.

Do not buy wrecked chassis. By the time all is said and done, it is better to buy a good used kart.

Turn the steering wheel and note if the steering shaft is bent. A slightly bent shaft usually does not cause problems, but it may be an indication of a previous crash.

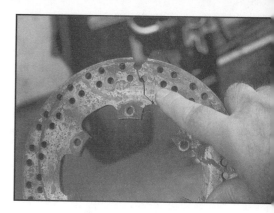

Look at the brake rotors closely for excess wear, rust and particularly cracks and breaks. Rotors are expensive and a lot of work to replace.

Grab the front wheels with both hands and check for play in the spindles and the bearings. Worn bearings can be easily replaced, but why buy something already worn out? With an LTO chassis check the weight jacker for play or rust.

Stand the kart on its rear bumper. Inspect the overall condition of the under tray.

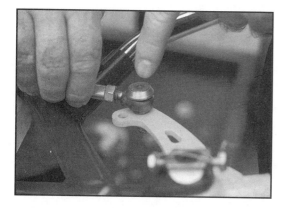

Inspect the tie rods and rod ends for wear, slop and cracks. Look if the tie rods are straight and of correct length.

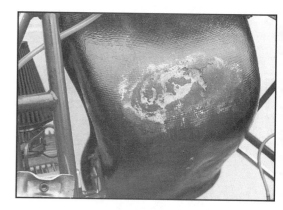

Check the condition of the seat bottom. In either dirt or asphalt racing the seats will show some signs of contact with the track. Minor damage can be repaired easily.

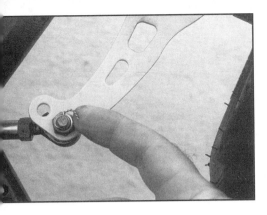

All the critical fasteners should be safety wired or cotter pinned. This would be a sign of care, otherwise you may be looking at a kart that has been thrown together from used parts laying around.

Peel back the brake master cylinder boot and inspect for leakage and rust.

Pay close attention to the welds and the steering column support tubes where they meet the main portion of the frame. This can be a weak spot on some karts.

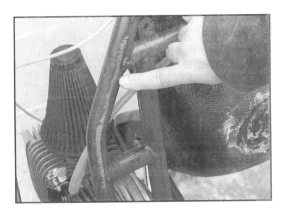

Chassis on asphalt will often show battle scars such as these. Some scratches are normal, but tubes worn flat or worse, worn through are not acceptable.

Spin the front wheels and listen for noisy wheel bearings. Check for warped wheels.

The belly pan fasteners often get worn flat by the chassis scraping on the track. Take a close look around the fasteners; belly pans often crack from this abuse. These are cheap parts, but difficult to replace.

Chapter 11
SCHOOLS, TRACKS, CLUBS & SHOPS
How to Make Friends and Influence People

KART RACING SCHOOLS

Most adults know how to drive a car. It would be logical then, to think that anyone can *drive* a racing kart. Yet *racing* a kart wheel to wheel with 10 or 20 other karts is vastly different from driving down the highway in the family wagon. Many novices make the mistake of thinking they can be competitive in a kart in their first race. Even those with extensive experience in other forms of racing will usually get beat in their first kart race. Racing a kart can be compared to playing golf: it looks easy watching someone else, but once you try to hold the club and hit the ball, it becomes a whole new ball game.

A karting school allows the newcomer to try the sport without investing a lot of money, and the schools teach the basics of karting before the new karter develops any bad habits. Some schools have "Arrive and Drive" programs the students can participate in after graduating. Again, this is another excellent opportunity to get into karting without investing in any equipment. An "Arrive and Drive" package also allows the student to ask questions and to learn how to setup the karts to be competitive. The "try before you buy" concept is a good one with karting.

A karting school can teach the basics of race driving and it allows the student to experience the feel of racing a kart at high speeds. When the new karter arrives at a race he will already have the basic knowledge of braking, turning, accelerating etc., and he will have learned the basics of taking the "lines". The lines in karting can be different from what experienced drivers in other forms of racing may be accustomed to.

A school will give the newbie a chance to learn at his own pace. Going fast comes from first going slow and working up to speed without making mistakes. Schools take the drivers through all the stages of speed and how to achieve it, one step at the time. In a race, there is the ever present pressure from the other competitors and the desire to look good and win. Pressure like this can be very detrimental. Many new karters try to win, instead of learning how to go fast. At a racing school there is no pressure and no one loses face; there are no losers, only winners.

Well-established shops carry a wide array of chassis models for all classes and ages.

chools play an invaluable role in karting. There ne drivers can learn the basics of racing, the flags, riving techniques, racing protocols, and courtesy. ome schools have their own specialties. Some oncentrate on dirt racing, while others like KRC in lendale, California, offer a curriculum for shifter arts.

Kart Racing Tracks

Kart tracks are plentiful throughout the U.S. nd Canada. Dirt and asphalt oval tracks are nore prevalent in the South, Southeast and lidwest, while asphalt Sprint tracks are at hand ll over the U.S. and Canada. Visit a track or wo in your area. Get a feel for the type of rac- ng they offer. Dirt and Sprint racing are vastly ifferent forms of karting. Both are fun, but they equire different driving techniques, equipment nd chassis setups and most importantly, each orm of racing fits different tastes and aspira- ions.

Some tracks offer practice time for those who vish to do some tuning and get accustomed to heir new mount. Many karters never race. Practice Karters" as they are known, just go ut and practice with their friends or family on n off race day at the local kart track. Some- imes a few friends get together and organize n impromptu race. Some "Practice Karters" nay get the urge to go out and see what they an do against the more experienced guys, and hey may enter the following race. Practice is n invaluable tool for the beginner and ad- anced karter alike.

A visit to a local track is an ideal occasion to btain a schedule of events and practice days.

Tracks in Canada and those east of the American Rockies are lush with greenery and vegetation. Dirt and asphalt tracks are well-groomed and maintained.

One might ask if the track has a school. Most tracks belong to one of the major karting orga- nizations, but many are "Outlaw Tracks" which run under their own rules and locate their own source for insurance.

While at the track, inquire if rentals are avail- able for a race day. The management may di- rect you to a shop or a school if they cannot oblige you. While at the track ask the questions you need to ask but remember that the racers may be busy with their kart. A visit on a prac- tice day may be better timing if you have a lot of questions to ask.

Track employees should be asked the fol- lowing questions:

Does track offer a school?
Is there a sound limit at the track?
Are there clubs at the track?
Are there practice days?

Dirt Tracks

In the U.S., dirt track racing ("Speedway") constitutes more than fifty percent of karting. Speedway offers excellent training grounds for the new karter. Dirt tracking is more prevalent east of the Rockies and it is most popular in the south and southeast. The Pedregon broth- ers, PJ and Page Jones began their racing ca- reers as dirt karters.

Dirt tracks are 1/10 mile to 1/4 mile in length and are made up of two left turns. The south- ern states are blessed with clay which retains the moisture to offer the best dirt racing pos- sible. Western states usually run on sand or cin- der, but some track owners have imported clay

Some schools offer Arrive and Drive programs with complete race series, including the opportunity for the winners to spray champagne over each other.

Dirt tracks require special care and maintenance. The southern and midwestern states are blessed with clay surfaces. The western states run on sand or cinder tracks, but many operators have imported clay from neighboring states.

Kart City Raceway near Las Vegas, Nevada, is typical of western tracks. Rocky terrain, snow-capped mountains in the winter and warm, breezy days in the summer, and lots of fun at night. Kart tracks are as diverse as the part of the continent they are in.

from neighboring states.

The first few laps of practice at a Speedway track are sometimes quite messy. The tracks are generously soaked with water to create a damp, dust-free tacky surface to provide traction throughout the race day. The first group of karts go out and "mud pack" to compact the muck and reduce the flying debris. Because of the need for water and the time required for grooming before racing, dirt tracks do not offer as much practice time as the Sprint tracks.

Dirt track racing boasts of ever changing track conditions, which provides excellent challenges to the drivers and pit crews in changing the chassis setup to keep up with the conditions.

Sprint Tracks

Sprint tracks range in length from 1/4 to 3/4 miles. The tracks' surface is generally concrete or asphalt and consists of right and left turns. The karts raced on these tracks are easily recognizable by the erect sitting position of the drivers and the slick tires. Each driver generally competes in two heats to determine the starting position and he receives some points for his finishing orders. The heat races determine the starting position for the main event which carries the majority of the points available for the race.

Sprint races are sometimes promoted on city streets. These events are known as "Street Races" and are increasing in popularity as city fathers realize the economic benefits of attracting thousands of people in their city walls. An increasing number of charities are also organizing street races to benefit their causes.

Clubs

Many clubs are run by the track management. The property owners can also put on their own events without being a bona fide club. When visiting your local track, inquire about the clubs that run there. The clubs will be best equipped to give you a list of rules and a list of engines which are run at their events. The club can fill you in on points such as:

- ❑ Schedule and time the gates open.
- ❑ Practice days and time.
- ❑ Classes, engine types, weights and age groups.
- ❑ Tire and fuel rules.
- ❑ Are there tracks and shops nearby?
- ❑ Does the club run Sprint, Road Racing or Speedway?

Talk to different clubs if you can. Sometimes there can be personality differences or there may be other factors such as scheduling or engines that are run which you may or may not like.

Attending a club meeting is also a good idea as it will introduce you to some of the members and get you involved with karting.

Many friendships have been created out of kart clubs. The clubs welcome the help of novices who want to learn and they always welcome volunteers to help carry out race day activities. As a flag man you will be allowed to get right on the edge of the track where you can pick up some driving techniques and learn the classes so you can decide which one is your favorite. As a volunteer you will get to know the "hot shoes" and you will gain access to the better equipment when it comes on the market.

Belonging to a club offers many advantages, one of which is the trophies which are awarded at the events. Clubs typically also have a year-end banquet to honor the participants and to reward the class winners.

The U.S. organizations hold yearly National Championships in all three divisions. The National Champions are crowned at banquets following the event. These trophies are the beginning of a long line of awards these young men will probably win.

The Associations set the rules for their members, sanction races, provide insurance to clubs and tracks, and put on National Championships each year. The members also receive a monthly publication which includes news and race results. The trophies in this photo are the Duffies awarded by the IKF to its National Champions. These trophies belong to Indy Car driver Richie Hearn.

ket. There are 175 clubs in the U.S. and 23 in Canada.

ASSOCIATIONS

The International Kart Federation (IKF) in Southern California, and the World Karting Association (WKA), based in North Carolina are the two major U.S. karting associations. Other regional sanctioning bodies in the U.S. include the Karters of America Racing Triad (KART). The triad represents the three divisions of karting, and the Pro Kart Challenge Association (PKCA) based in the north east. In Canada, the ASN Canada FIA is the principal karting organization. In all other countries, kart racing is governed by the Commission Internationale de Karting (CIK) a division of the Federation Internationale de l'Automobile (FIA). The CIK is based in Switzerland.

While most clubs use rules which are derived from the IKF or WKA, there may be some

Clubs supply tech inspectors to enforce the rules and keep the racing fair. Most clubs follow IKF's or WKA's rules. Both Associations' rules are very similar.

differences between clubs and organizations. These differences are known as "local options" and these can differ from track to track to satisfy local preferences. The most common difference is with the tire rules, whereby some clubs or divisions of the sanctioning organizations vote to run "spec" tires. Classes with such rules make good entry levels.

IKF, WKA and KART offer memberships which entitle the members to an annual rule book, membership card, driving suit patch and a monthly magazine. It is advisable to join at least one of the organizations, as they supply race schedules for the big national events. Membership is mandatory to race in the big national events sanctioned by the organizations.

KART SHOPS

Karting is a sport and a business. As a racer you will be involved in the sport. The kart shops are involved in the business aspect. Like in any other business, time is money and shops do not make any money giving away information. A cold fact? Yes, but real.

The best time to approach a shop is midweek. Mondays are hectic because the regular customers bring back their motors and chassis for repairs and maintenance. Fridays are filled with last minute jobs for the weekend races. Reading this book and following the steps outlined in it will go a long way toward cutting your time spent asking questions. Try to adhere to the questions outlined in this book and have a list ready when you go to the shop. Use the

Trophies and memorabilia are a good sign that a shop has been in business for a while and that they take the sport and the industry seriously. Some shops, such as JM Racing, have ties with Indy Car and Formula 1 drivers and teams. This makes for a good place to start karting. Photo courtesy JM Racing.

The greater the number of services the shop offers, the better the shop is. Buller Built in Henderson, Nebraska, builds two- and four-cycles and the shop also does dyno testing, engine and carburetor blueprinting, and flow bench work.

Kart shops should keep an ample stock of the tires and chassis parts commonly used in the area. The shop should be able to order tires for the karters who travel to race on tracks with different tire regulations.

lists in chapters 9 and 12.

Most kart shops will be eager to answer your questions, but remember to patronize the shop and to thank the employees for their help. Their assistance will probably be needed again.

Locating a Kart Shop

Look for kart shops in the phone book under "Go-Karts". Referrals can be obtained at a

Better shops carry a wide variety of helmets and driving suits, new and used karts and engines, lubricants, and tools. In short, a kart shop is a one-stop shop if someone is going karting.

track, or from the clubs. At least one karting oriented business per state and per province (if available) is listed in the back of this book. The karting publications also carry advertisements for many shops. The Association magazines and particularly their rule book issue include many suppliers and advertisers.

Good kart shops will have been established for some time, they take credit cards and they will be open during normal business hours.

Legitimate shops have a store front and a business address, they carry insurance and the necessary licenses. You may get a deal from some backyard operation once or twice, but you will not get the service, warranty and convenience you deserve.

Look at the brand names the shop carries. The larger shops will carry several well known names. You can check the brand names in the ads in the karting magazines. The principal advantage to this is the parts availability, and the larger companies will make the latest developments, setups and technology available to their bigger customers first. The information will, in turn, get imparted to the customers when they stop by the shop. Ask if the shop races and if it has won any championships, especially Nationals.

Shop around, but don't over do it. Karting is a hobby to you, to the shops it is a business. Convenience, good advice and an honest, sincere shop owner is usually more important than price. Once you find a shop or engine builder you feel comfortable with, stick with him. Loyalty is a two-way street.

Decisions, decisions. This newbie is getting his money's worth just by dealing with a kart shop. Shop employees know the local trends, the engines and type of tracks they are raced on. This type of knowledge can be invaluable to a newcomer.

All these guys need is a potbellied stove, a pickle barrel, and a deck of cards. Some bench racing goes on in kart shops, but remember that the shops are in karting as a business. Cal Kart/ Invader in San Jose, California, is one of the oldest kart shops in the country.

STEP 1

Read *Karting! A Complete Introduction* for the U.S. and Canada. Follow the lists and take notes.

STEP 2

First trip to shop:

Ask the shop owner the type of karting most common in the area.

Inquire as to the types of engines used at local tracks.

Find out where the local tracks are.

Ask about local club rules, and where they race.

Fill out the lists in chapters 9 and 12 as you go.

STEP 3

Visit some tracks:

Decide on the division you prefer based on your preferences and the availability of tracks and clubs.

Decide on the type of engine you prefer (two-or four-cycle) based on availability of classes and cost of parts, ease of tuning and simplicity.

Decide the class you would most like to run.

Ask the following questions while at the track:

Is it an Oval dirt or asphalt, or a Sprint track?

Does track offer a school?

Is there an exhaust noise limit at the track?

Are there practice days?

Are there clubs at the track?

Which engines are raced at the track?

The clubs can fill you in on points such as:

Schedule and time the gates open.

Practice days and time.

Classes, engine types, weights and age groups.

Tire and fuel rules.

Does the club run Sprint, Road Racing or Speedway?

Directions to tracks.

STEP 4

Fill out the following list, take it to your kart shop and discuss it with the staff:

Age of driver:

Weight and height:

Division preferred:

Engine (two-or four-cycle):

Class preferred:

New or used engine?:

New or used kart?:

STEP 5

Check the parts you need and take list to kart shop to purchase what you need to get started. Ask shop owner if he has any suggestions for other parts and tools.

Parts from the kart shop:

❏ Battery charger
❏ Chain
❏ Chain breaker
❏ Chain oiler for dirt racing
❏ Clutch tools
❏ Cotter pins
❏ Duct tape
❏ Engine
❏ Fire extinguisher
❏ Fuel jug
❏ Funnel and filter
❏ Gears
❏ Gloves
❏ Goggles
❏ Helmet
❏ Helmet and gear bag
❏ Jets (four-cycle)
❏ Kart
❏ Lead
❏ Neck collar
❏ Numbers and panels
❏ Ratio Rite
❏ Rule book
❏ Shoes
❏ Spark plugs
❏ Stand
❏ Starter and battery
❏ Stopwatch
❏ Suit
❏ Tear Offs (Speedway dirt)
❏ Throttle cable and stay
❏ Tires
❏ Tie-straps

Chemicals and Lubricants from the kart shop

❏ Air filter cleaner and oil
❏ Alcohol fuel lubricant (methanol classes)
❏ Brake fluid
❏ Chain lube
❏ Clutch oil
❏ Fuel
❏ Hand cleaner

Better shops carry quality products and are proud to display the companies' decals on their karts' bodywork.

Better shops are clean, well-lit, and stocked with all the parts and equipment you may need.

- ❏ Motor oil
- ❏ Pre-mix
- ❏ Solvent cleaner
- ❏ Thread locker
- ❏ Wheel bearing grease

Basic Tools

- ❏ Compression gauge
- ❏ Feeler gauges
- ❏ Plug wrench
- ❏ Tire pump or air tank
- ❏ T-handled Allen wrenches (metric or U.S. depending on chassis and engine), snap ring pliers, screwdrivers, tape measure, wire cutters, needle nose pliers, pliers, files, hammer, hack saw and blades, extensions, a small and a large adjustable wrench. Box end/open end combination wrenches and socket set in either metric or standard.

Use the following guidelines and considerations in choosing an engine.

- ❏ Is the replacement parts cost of the engine you are contemplating acceptable?
- ❏ Are those engines raced on tracks within an acceptable driving distance?
- ❏ Are there builders in your area who can service the engine and supply parts?
- ❏ Is it a late model with a wide local following?
- ❏ How easy to tune is it? Consider the clutch, exhaust, carburetor and gearing.
- ❏ Look at the typical maximum RPM the engines turn in their class.
- ❏ Is the engine blueprinted, or is it stock? Does it need freshening?
- ❏ Look for value, not just price.
- ❏ Who built the engine, and who maintained it?
- ❏ Does the engine use metric or standard fasteners?
- ❏ A four-cycle does not require a fuel tank, third bearing support and its clutch and exhaust system are less expensive than two-cycles. Two-strokes generally require an air box.

Use the following guidelines and considerations when choosing a chassis.

- ❏ How long has the manufacturer been in business?
- ❏ Are the parts available from dealers without goi[ng] through the importer?
- ❏ Does the manufacturer or importer have a solid h[is]tory?
- ❏ Do you fit comfortably in the seat and kart?
- ❏ Initial cost and price of replacement parts.
- ❏ Will the chassis fit in the division of karting you a[re] planning on entering.
- ❏ Will the chassis accept the engine you are planni[ng] on running?

Tips on Choosing a Helmet

- ❏ Choose a quality full face helmet.
- ❏ Try on a few different types of helmets.
- ❏ Choose a helmet which is on the snug side when ne[w]
- ❏ Never buy a used helmet.
- ❏ Do not buy a child too large a helmet hoping he w[ill] grow into it.
- ❏ Buy a helmet with at least the latest Snell rating.
- ❏ Try on the goggles, face shield and/or, glasses if y[ou] wear any.
- ❏ Think comfort.

Points to Ponder

- ❏ Consider the age of the person you are looking [at] karting for.
- ❏ Physical condition and conditioning also require r[e]flection.
- ❏ Marital status and age of children.
- ❏ Financial situation.
- ❏ Time available to travel.
- ❏ Space to work on the kart.
- ❏ Transportation available to get to the track.
- ❏ What hobbies do you currently have?
- ❏ Have you been involved in other forms of motorspor[t] in the past?
- ❏ How long have you wanted to race?

Points To Consider

- ❏ Who are you looking at karting for? Yourself, chil[d,] spouse?
- ❏ Do you prefer road type racing, or Oval track?
- ❏ If Oval track, do you prefer dirt or asphalt?
- ❏ Do you prefer two- or four-cycle engines?
- ❏ Type of kart you need: Cadet, Enduro, Sprint, Ov[al] asphalt or dirt, Shifter?
- ❏ Club and Association to join.
- ❏ Class you want to race in.
- ❏ Do you want to buy new or used?
- ❏ Accessories and tools you will need.

FREQUENTLY ASKED QUESTIONS

Q: What kind of tires are used in karting?

A: The tires are dictated by the availability from manufacturers, the type of karting the tires are used in and the rules. For example, a dirt track may dictate a certain brand tire of specified dimensions. Dirt racing requires grooved tires and Sprint and Road Racing uses slicks and rain tires when applicable. Some Sprint clubs also have a tire rule which dictates a brand and compound. Asphalt tracks are raced on with slick tires and dirt tracks favor grooved tires. Always use tires rated for racing.

Q: What type of engines are used?

A: In the U.S. and Canada two and four-cycles are used. The engines are single cylinder, and for the most part they are air cooled. The beginner is strongly advised to remain with engines which are widely available, those which are used in national classes, the engines which are easy to tune, low maintenance and motors whose parts are relatively inexpensive.

Q: What types of karting are the most popular in the U.S. and Canada?

A: Sprint is the most ubiquitous form of karting in the U.S. and Canada. In the U.S., karting is also practiced on dirt and asphalt oval tracks.

Q: What type of racing is most popular, dirt or sprint?

A: The number of dirt karters is probably slightly larger than the Sprint drivers. Each form of karting is more or less popular in different parts of the country, with dirt racing being more prevalent in the south and south-east of the U.S., while Sprint is more prevalent in other parts of America. In Canada Sprint karting is the major form of karting.

Q: Can I just go practice without racing?

A: Absolutely. Many racers have started in "practice karting", others simply enjoy driving a high powered kart around a twisty track with their friends and family.

Q: I want a kart I can drive on the parking lot.

A: This practice is not recommended for safety and legal reasons. Furthermore, racing clutches are not made to operate at sustained low speeds. A "fun kart" would be more appropriate for recreational driving, but a helmet and all the safety equipment should still be worn and karts may not be driven on private properties, or on city streets and alleys.

Q: Schools, clubs, tracks nearby?

A: There are tracks and clubs in all parts of Canada and the U.S.A. Your local kart shop can give you more specific information for your locality.

Q: How fast do they go?

A: Some karts can reach speeds of up to 140 miles-per-hour. The average kart on a dirt track will reach 40 to 50 miles-per-hour. Beginners are best served in classes where the top speed is in the moderate range.

Q: How old do you have to be?

A: Some clubs and tracks have classes starting at 4 to 6 years of age. Most Junior classes allow drivers who have attained the age of 8.

Q: When does the season start?

A: In the colder regions karters can get cabin fever; the season starts the minute the snow ha cleared off the track. Most kart clubs in parts of the U.S. and Canada with clement weathe run races all year around, with a break around the end of fall through the first of the year

Q: Are there rental programs?

A: Some shops, schools and tracks have rentals and "arrive and drive" programs. Ask you local kart shop if they know of rentals in your area.

Q: Can I sit in the kart?

A: It is an excellent idea to sit in a kart you are contemplating on buying to ensure that th seat, the steering, and pedals fit the driver properly.

Q: What class should a novice start in?

A: Classes for a novice should be first determined based on the age of the driver, and the simplicity and the budget of the driver. The novice should also consider the availability c the class he prefers. Choose the division of karting that appeals to you most (oval or Sprint then choose an engine type (2- or 4-cycle) and finally pick your class.

SUPPLIERS

labama

UNT'S KART SALES	(205) 547-7506
M'S SMALL ENGINE AND KART SHOP	(205) 675-2357
ARTER BROTHERS MFG INC	(800) 523-5278

rizona

DVANCED RACING	(305) 463-5278
RIZONA COMPETITION KARTS	(520) 579-8766
RAND PRIX RACING	(602) 279-4588
LEMENTS RACING PRODUCTS	(602) 684-2933
OB BONDURANT SCHOOL	(800) 842-7223

alifornia

KS MANUFACTURING	(209) 251-4226
IGHREV ENGINEERING	(209) 251-4835
PEX RACING SCHOOL	(310) 541-3430
ELSON MANUFACTURING	(408) 263-4334
AL KART	(408) 293-3702
URPHY BROTHERS RACING	(408) 449-1488
&C KART SHOP	(408) 842-3060
RACK MAGIC RACING	(415) 822-6795
DH KARTING EQUIPMENT	(510) 417-1981
URRIS MANUFACTURING	(562) 493-2031
AVE TURNER MOTORSPORTS	(619) 571-3811
ZUSA ENGINEERING	(626) 967-4167
&P MANUFACTURING	(626) 334-0334
M RACING INC	(626) 446-5443
EARN COMPETITION KARTING	(626) 574-0890
OHN'S GO KARTS AND ACCESSORIES	(707) 546-8823
ED LINE SYNTHETIC OIL	(707) 745-6100
AMAHA OF AMERICA	(714) 523-3963
AMAHA MOTOR CORPORATION USA	(800) 889-2624
ORSTMAN MANUFACTURING	(760) 598-2100
NERGY KARTS	(760) 804-9087
SC RACING	(760) 864-1320
DAMS KART TRACK	(800) 350-3826
ACE KART ENGINEERING	(800) 527-8377
IKE MANNING KARTING	(805) 256-7500
IM HALL RACING INC	(805) 654-1329
&T MANUFACTURING	(626) 334-6800
ART RACING CO	(818) 507-1436
ITTS PERFORMANCE	(818) 780-2184
NTL. KARTING FEDERATION	(909) 625-5497
MMICK ENTERPRISES INC.	(916) 383-2288
ERRY IVES INDUSTRIES	(916) 725-6776
WO WILD	(949) 470-1940

olorado

UN ENTERPRISES	(303) 287-7566
KE MOTORSPORTS	(303) 371-5427

Connecticut

BONES KART SHOP	(203) 783-9925
PRO KART RACE TUNED KARTS	(860) 290-9091

Delaware

STALLARD CHASSIS	(302) 292-1800

Florida

T.S. RACING	(352) 793-9600
LIGHTNING RACING PRODUCTS	(407) 352-2260
HSP HIGH SPEED PRODUCTS	(407) 831-1426
PRIMUS RACING—HAASE USA	(813) 522-7544
KARTING INNOVATIONS INC	(904) 761-2427

Georgia

TNC KART MART	(404) 474-4408
SPEED BY JONES	(706) 754-7190
KENNESAW KART SHOP	(770) 926-9202
BOLINK R/C CARS	(770) 963-0252
DEALER'S SUPPLY CO.	(800) 241-6050
AMUNDSEN RESEARCH CORP	(800) 521-3560
BRANTLEY RACING ENGINES	(800) 588-2414
STUDIER KART SUPPLY	(912) 772-3876

Hawaii

NKT RACING	(808) 528-0048

Iowa

THE INSIDE TRACK	(319) 472-4763
WALLER RACING	(319) 478-2773
TURK BROTHERS RACING	(515) 424-4321
VAN HAAFTEN RACING INC	(515) 627-5081
MARSHALTOWN IOWA INT. RACEWAY	(515) 753-6362
UNCLE FRANK'S 4-CYCLE RACING SPEC	(712) 322-6664

Idaho

BEAUDRY MOTORSPORTS	(800) 735-2407

Illinois

JAY LUPO RACING ENTERPRISES	(216) 731-6095
S&M KART SUPPLY	(217) 546-9120
LAUKAITIS RACING	(217) 877-8877
MAROON'S KART SYSTEMS	(309) 637-5278
PROFESSIONAL KARTING ASSO.	(573) 393-2458
EVANS BROTHERS RACING ENGINES	(630) 393-3886
PROFILE RACING	(630) 628-1973
GEM PRODUCTS LTD	(630) 653-1800
KART MARKETING GROUP	(630) 653-7368
MRP RACING SCHOOL	(708) 234-6357
L.A.D. SPECIALTIES	(708) 430-1588
JOHN'S KART SHOP	(773) 586-5600
CHICAGO KARTING TECHNOLOGY	(773) 725-3825
BOB'S KART SHOP	(815) 496-2820

Indiana

KARTER'S PIT STOP INC	(219) 262-9571
NATIONAL KART NEWS	(219) 277-0033
ELROB RACING KARTS	(219) 663-6575
STALLION RACING PRODUCTS	(219) 884-0628
JASON'S KART SHOP	(317) 247-8367
CARLSON RACING ENGINES/VECTOR MFG	(317) 339-4407
BURGESS MOTORSPORTS	(317) 398-2016
COMET KART SALES	(317) 462-3413
FOX VALLEY KART SHOP	(317) 742-0935
WHITE CHASSIS RACING KARTS INC	(317) 838-9133
EDDIE'S KART SALES	(317) 962-7951
MARKER KART PART	(800) 300-1255
ELLIOTT MOTORSPORTS	(812) 235-0846
EBERTS KART RACING	(812) 392-2226
SCOTTY'S PRO KARTS	(812) 752-6257
BRIAN'S KART SHOP	(812) 882-6724

Kansas

MIDWEST KART LLC	(316) 744-1687
CFOM MOTORSPORTS INC	(913) 379-0496

Kentucky

BKR KARTS AND PARTS	(502) 684-2544
A-1 KARTS & PARTS	(502) 957-3818

Louisiana

ROCKET RACING INC	(318) 343-1421
GO KARTS PLUS	(318) 938-5278

Massachusetts

COMPETITION KART SALES	(413) 283-2260
DINO USA	(508) 670-8122
ALL KART INTERNATIONAL	(617) 471-2282

Maryland

KART CONNECTION PLUS	(301) 620-7501
ROBINSON SPEED SHOP	(410) 835-2183

Michigan

STONEY CREEK MOTORSPORTS	(313) 697-6971
MICHIGAN KART SUPPLY	(517) 663-2200
RIVER CITY SPEEDWAY	(517) 895-7223
LEAF RACEWEAR	(519) 659-1115
GREAT LAKES KART COMPANY	(616) 399-2336
MRP/SPEED	(616) 422-2926
NEEDLES RACING ENGINES	(616) 429-3345
GREAT LAKES DISTRIBUTOR	(800) 372-8612
GREAT LAKES MOTORSPORTS	(810) 233-7811

Minnesota

RIVERLAKE RACING	(612) 729-7589
GOODSON AUTO MACHINE	(800) 533-8010

Missouri

BAUER RACING ENGINES	(314) 225-886
ST LOUIS KARTING MOTORS	(314) 645-347
MARGAY RACING PRODUCTS	(314) 771-424
BISHCO SALES KARTING	(417) 865-579
FTZ PERFORMANCE INC	(573) 334-543
KANSAS CITY KART SUPPLY	(800) 455-065
RUSSELL KARTING SPECIALTIES	(800) 821-335
K.A.R.T. INC	(816) 331-877
FAIRFIELD MOTORSPORTS	(816) 836-680

Mississippi

LIGHTNING RACING PRODUCTS	(601) 773-939

North Carolina

MISHUE MOTORSPORTS	(336) 766-792
PIEDMONT KART SHOP	(704) 256-658
RICK LITTLE PERFORMANCE RACING	(704) 291-782
SPEED KARTS INC	(704) 334-010
RACE FEST MOTORSPORTS SHOW	(704) 347-879
WORLD KARTING ASSOCIATION	(704) 455-160
GOODSON RACING ENGINES	(704) 637-7458
CHECKERED FLAG FUELS	(704) 784-333
WIGGINS KART SHOP/PHANTOM CHAS.	(704) 855-316
CENTRAL HIGH PERFORMANCE	(800) 222-680
CV PRODUCTS	(800) 874-122
TRUE VALUE KART CENTER	(910) 488-555
STEVENS MOTORSPORTS	(910) 593-301
BORDEAUX DYNO CAMS	(910) 655-903
COMPETITION KARTING INC	(910) 731-611
BEEF PERFORMANCE RACING	(910) 983-381
G&S KARTS AND PARTS	(919) 779-160

Nebraska

BULLER BUILT	(402) 723-471

New Hampshire

RIC RACING ENGINES	(603) 224-9264
ARCHAMBAULT RACING KARTS	(603) 465-7638

New Jersey

EURO KART RACING INTERNATIONAL	(201) 794-362
TOP END MOTORSPORT	(908) 281-792
RAMPARTS INC	(908) 362-9137
KUSTOM KART RACING	(908) 477-686
BUTLER-BUILT RACERS	(908) 725-339

New Mexico

EEI RACE KARTS	(505) 527-066

Nevada

RACE KART CITY RACEWAY	(702) 260-6455
RC ENGINES	(702) 322-9481
KARTWERKS SPEED & SPORTS	(702) 348-9040
BONSIGNORE KART SUPPLY	(516) 243-5220
BENNETT MOTOR SALES	(607) 547-9332
MIDWEST KARTING PERFORMANCE	(614) 855-0100
COYOTE PRODUCTS	(716) 352-0806
MXK RACING	(716) 674-9494
VES MOTORSPORTS	(905) 529-4287

Ohio

LAKE ERIE MOTORSPORTS	(216) 257-9000
AMERICAN POWER SPORTS	(216) 564-8100
OTS RACING PRODUCTS	(440) 293-4070
DEIS RACING ENGINES	(513) 274-3518
MOSSBARGER RACING PRODUCTS	(513) 642-2027
PKP KARTING PRODUCTS	(513) 743-4433
ADKINS SPEED CENTER	(614) 498-5157

Oklahoma

POLE POSITION RACING ENGINES	(405) 340-8986
KART WERKS LLC	(405) 478-3380
PRO KART	(405) 752-0159

Oregon

PFAU DIST. WORLD OF KARTING	(503) 283-1026
KNIGHT KART SUPPLY	(503) 666-4307

Pennsylvania

GRAND PRODUCTS	(215) 244-1940
KNIGHT PERFORMANCE	(412) 342-4677
DT RACING	(610) 532-5037
SHUPP'S KART SHOP INC	(610) 759-1140

South Carolina

PREDATOR KART MFG.	(803) 329-2629
SPECTER RACING CHASSIS	(803) 399-4132
SHADOW KARTS	(803) 794-7247
SOX AND SONS	(803) 794-7247
DAVIS MANUFACTURING CO.	(803) 839-5166
DRIGGERS SMALL ENGINES	(803) 875-1421
DIXIE KARTING INC	(864) 294-8417
DILL FABRICATION	(864) 322-0504
CAROLINA SPEED SHOP	(864) 467-1144

South Dakota

ROBERTSON'S TORQUE TUBES	(605) 584-1775

Tennessee

BADGER RACING/PROTOTYPE ENGIN.	(423) 538-5849
HADDOCK LTD	(423) 698-0847
S & O SALES	(423) 927-5906
COMPETITION CAMS INC	(800) 976-9376
E-RACER KARTS	(901) 388-1559

Texas

MOTO LIBERTY INC—HRC ENGINES	(214) 242-6440
PRECISION KARTING	(214) 243-0714
PITSTOP PERFORMANCE PROD. INC.	(713) 947-3373
CHRISTIAN'S AUTOMOTIVE	(806) 747-2553

Virginia

GRIFFITH SPECIALTIES	(540) 433-2408
TOMMY'S KARTS AND PARTS	(804) 372-5579

Washington

KART RACING COOPERATIVE	(206) 531-7815
BAM RACING LTD.	(206) 778-8992
SHIFT KART	(425) 672-8806
PETE'S KART SHOP INC	(509) 662-2449
ITALIAN MOTORS	(800) 330-5278

Wisconsin

BRIGGS & STRATTON CORP, IND DIV.	(414) 259-5333
TECUMSEH MOTRSPORTS DIVISION	(414) 377-2700
TWO CYCLE TECHNOLOGY	(414) 628-2438
COELLO RACING	(414) 650-0450

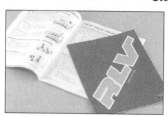

Computer Inventory for the BEST Mail Order Service in the Karting

Shop Online at
www.TSRacing.com
Karting's SuperStore

Finally, an E-Store that is Fast, Easy & Secure

TS Racing is one of the largest warehouse distributors for all of kartings' biggest manufacturers. If you don't see a specific item in our catalog just ask, we probably have it or can get it for you. Our staff is well versed in all aspects of karting from dirt to asphalt, sprint to enduro, two and four cycle. Don't forget we also build killer engines (over 100 National Titles).

FREE
Kart Racing Catalog #5
140+ pages of products

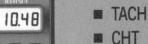

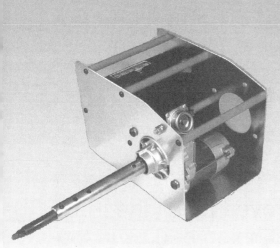
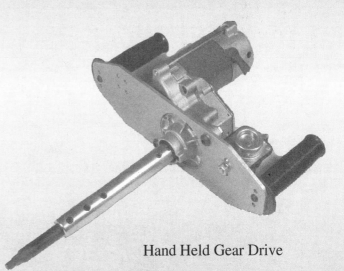

YAMAHA

KT100S

"THE LEADER IN KART RACING"

- Approved by all the major sanctioning bodies in the United States, Canada and Mexico.

- More National Championship titles have been won with the Yamaha KT100S.

- Over 130 dealers ready to provide support with genuine Yamaha spare parts.

To locate your nearest authorized Yamaha kart engine dealer call, or visit our website.

United States:	1-800-6-YAMAHA	www.yamaha-motor.com
Canada:	1-800-267-8577	www.yamaha-motor.ca
Mexico:	5 565-4453	

One for the
OVAL

One for the
ROAD

Raptor3

ANIMAL

With Briggs & Stratton you've got options! The 206cc "flathead" RAPTOR racing engine is the standard of oval racing, and has been for years and years. The brand new cool-running 206cc "OHV" ANIMAL engine is destined to revolutionize road racing with it's potential for extreme power combined with huge torque and low maintenance. Check out the details at www.briggsracing.com or through www.briggsandstratton.com. For use in sanctioned events only.

Nobody builds more engines for more kinds of *racing* than *Briggs & Stratton*

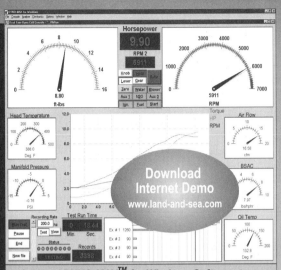
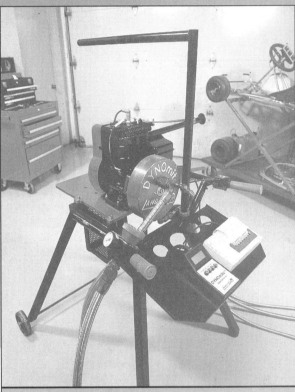